# The Three Peaks
## and the
# Howgill Fells

## Sheila Bowker

**Series editor Andrew Bibby**

FREEDOM TO ROAM

FRANCES LINCOLN

My passion for mountains and wilderness has been passed down to me by my father, Malcolm Bowker, and it is to him that this book is dedicated.

The Freedom to Roam guides are dedicated to the memory of Benny Rothman

Frances Lincoln Ltd
4 Torriano Mews
Torriano Avenue
London NW5 2RZ
www.franceslincoln.com

*The Three Peaks and the Howgill Fells*
Copyright © Sheila Bowker 2006

Photographs on frontispiece, pages 12–13, 16–17, 22–3, 34–5, 58–9, 74–5, 82–3, 92–3, 154–5 © John Morrison; photographs on pages 27, 44–5, 55, 64–5, 103, 113, 124–5, 132–3, 143 © Sheila Bowker; photograph on page 49 © Jeff Cowling, Craven Pothole Club; photograph on page 57 by Peter Wakely © English Nature; photograph on page 67 © English Nature; photograph on page 105 Unnetie Digital Archive © North Yorkshire County Council; photograph on page 117 © Historical Model Railway Society/N Wilkinson; photograph on page 135 by Kevin Cook © Cumbria Wildlife Trust; photograph on page 147 © Ingleton Community Centre; illustration on page 160 © Martin Bagness

Lyrics from 'The Manchester Rambler' song by Ewan MacColl used by kind permission of Peggy Seeger and of the publisher Harmony Music Ltd. Lyrics from 'The Settle to Carlisle' and 'Land of the Old and Grey' by Mike Donald used by kind permission of Pauline Donald. Lyrics from 'The Sleeping Lion' by Robert Dugdale, 'A picture of Settle' by Sue MacKay and 'Dry Stone Wallers Song' by Pip Grimes used by kind permission of the songwriters.

Reproduced by permission of Ordnance Survey on behalf of HMSO. © Crown Copyright 2005. All rights reserved. Ordnance Survey Licence number 100043293.

First published by Frances Lincoln 2006

British Library Cataloguing in Publication Data
A catalogue record for this book is available from the British Library

ISBN 0-7112-2555-9
Printed and bound in Singapore by Kyodo Printing Co.
9 8 7 6 5 4 3 2 1

*Frontispiece photograph:* Ingleborough from Kingsdale

# Contents

# Before you go – a checklist

- *Are access-land restrictions in place?*
  Access land may be subject to temporary or permanent restrictions. Check at
  www.countrysideaccess.gov.uk or on 0845 100 3298.

- *Are weather conditions appropriate?*
  When poor weather is forecast, it may be sensible to postpone some of the
  walks in this book.

- *Do you have suitable equipment?*
  High ground can be significantly colder and more exposed than valley areas. A
  map and compass are recommended.

- *Does someone know where you are going?*
  If walking in a remote area, it is a good idea to leave details of your route and
  time of return.

- *Do you want to take a dog?*
  In general, you should assume that you will *not* be able to take dogs on open
  country. Most of the moors covered by this book have dog-exclusion orders in
  place. Check on the website or helpline given above.

- *Are birds nesting?*
  Between March and June open country is home to many ground-nesting birds.
  To find out where conservation restrictions are in force, check on the website
  or helpline given above.

# Acknowledgements

The author gratefully acknowledges the assistance given her by a wide range of
individuals and organizations, and is especially grateful for the help offered by
Andrew Bibby, the series editor, and by Fiona Robertson at Frances Lincoln. The
assistance given by the following is also much appreciated: Steve Hastie (area
ranger, Yorkshire Dales National Park Authority); Ian Court (species officer,
Yorkshire Dales National Park Authority); John Osborne (English Nature); Simon
Lloyds (Red Alert North West, Cumbria Wildlife Trust); Dr Kate Wilshaw (limestone
pavement and planning officer, Cumbria Wildlife Trust); Frank Lee (projects
officer, Friends of the Lake District); Pip Grimes and Sue Mackay (Settle Voices);
Bill Noble and Robert Dugdale (Farmstead); Pauline Donald; W.R. Mitchell MBE;
Phil Hudson; Edmund and Henry Morphet; Dr John Hamilton; Robert Hordern; Jill
Sykes; Mary Corder; Robert Bell; Michael Faraday; Sheila Knowles; Pip Rigby;
Matthew Bayes; John Morrison; George Gooch.

# Series introduction

This book, and the companion books in the series, celebrate the arrival in England and Wales of the legal right to walk in open country. The title for the series is borrowed from a phrase much used during the long campaign for this right – Freedom to Roam. For years, it was the dream of many to be able to walk at will across mountain top, moorland and heath, free of the risk of being confronted by a 'Keep Out' sign or being turned back by a gamekeeper.

The sense of frustration that the hills were, in many cases, out of bounds to ordinary people was captured in the song 'The Manchester Rambler' written by one of the best-known figures in Britain's post-war folk revival, Ewan MacColl. The song, which was inspired by the 1932 'mass trespass' on Kinder Scout when walkers from Sheffield and Manchester took to the forbidden Peak District hills, tells the tale of an encounter between a walker, trespassing on open land, and an irate gamekeeper:

*He called me a louse, and said 'Think of the grouse',*
*Well I thought but I still couldn't see*
*Why old Kinder Scout, and the moors round about,*
*Couldn't take both the poor grouse and me.*

The desire, as Ewan MacColl expressed it, was a simple one:

*So I'll walk where I will, over mountain and hill*
*And I'll lie where the bracken is deep,*
*I belong to the mountains, the clear running fountains*
*Where the grey rocks rise ragged and steep.*

Some who loved the outdoors and campaigned around the time of the Kinder Scout trespass in the 1930s must have thought that the legal right to walk in open country would be won after the Second World War, at the time when the national parks were being created and the rights-of-way network drawn up. It was not to be. It was another half century before, finally, Parliament passed the Countryside and Rights of Way Act 2000, and the people of England and Wales gained the legal right to take to the hills and the moors. (Scotland has its own traditions and its own legislation.)

We have dedicated this series to the memory of Benny Rothman, one of the leaders of the 1932 Kinder Scout mass trespass who was imprisoned for his part in what was deemed a 'riotous assembly'. Later in his life, Benny Rothman was a familiar figure at rallies called by the Ramblers' Association as once again the issue of access rights came to the fore. But we should pay tribute to all who have campaigned for this goal. Securing greater access to the countryside was one of the principles on which the Ramblers' Association was founded in 1935, and for many ramblers the access legislation represents the achievement of literally a lifetime of campaigning.

So now, at last, we do have freedom to roam. For the first time in several centuries, the open mountains, moors and heaths of England and Wales are open for all. We have the protected right to get our boots wet in the peat bogs, to flounder in the tussocks, to blunder and scrabble through the bracken and heather, and to discover countryside which, legally, we had no way of knowing before.

The Freedom to Roam series of books has one aim: to encourage you to explore and grow to love these new areas of the countryside which are now open to us. The right to roam freely – that's surely something to celebrate.

*Andrew Bibby*
*Series editor*

# Walking in open country – a guide to using this book

If the right and the freedom to roam openly are so important – perceptive readers may be asking – why produce a set of books to tell you where to go?

So a word of explanation about this series. The aim is certainly not to encourage walkers to follow each other, ant-like, over the hills, sticking rigidly to a pre-determined itinerary. We are not trying to be prescriptive, instructing you on your walk stile by stile or gate by gate. The books are not intended as instruction manuals but we hope that they will be valuable as *guides* – helping you discover areas of the countryside which you haven't legally walked on before, advising you on routes you might want to take and telling you about places of interest you will be passing along the way.

In places where it can be tricky to find routes or track down landmarks, we offer more detailed instructions.

Elsewhere, we are deliberately less precise in our directions, allowing you to choose your own particular path or line to follow. For each walk, however, there is a recommended core route, and this forms the basis on which the distances given are calculated.

There is, then, an assumption that those who use this book will be comfortable with using a map – and that, in practice, means one of the Ordnance Survey's 1:25 000 Explorer series of maps. As well as referring to the maps in this book, it is worth taking the full OS map with you, to give you a wider picture of the countryside you will be exploring.

## Safety in the hills

Those who are already experienced upland walkers will not be surprised if at this point we put in a note on basic safety in the hills.

Walkers need to remember that walking in open country, particularly high country, is different from footpath walking across farmland or more gentle countryside. The main risk for walkers is of being inadequately prepared for changes in the weather. Even in high summer, hail and even snow are not impossible. Daniel Defoe found this out in August 1724 when he crossed the Pennines from Rochdale, leaving a calm clear day behind to find himself almost lost in a blizzard on the tops.

If rain comes the temperature will drop as well, so it is important to be properly equipped when taking to the hills and to guard against the risk of hypothermia. Fortunately, walkers today have access to a range of wind- and rain-proof clothing which was not available in the eighteenth century. Conversely, in hot weather you should take sufficient water to avoid the risk of dehydration and hyperthermia (dangerous overheating of the body).

Be prepared for visibility to drop when (to use the local term) the clag descends on the hills. It is always sensible to take a compass. If you are unfamiliar with basic compass-and-map work, ask in a local outdoor equipment shop whether they have simple guides available or pick the brains of a more experienced walker.

The other main hazard, even for walkers who know the hills well, is that of suffering an accident such as a broken limb. If you plan to walk alone, it is sensible to let someone know in advance where you will be walking and when you expect to be back – the moorland and mountain rescue services which operate in the area covered by this book are very experienced but they are not psychic. Groups of walkers should tackle only what the least experienced or least fit member of the party can comfortably achieve. Take particular care if you intend to take children with you to hill country. And take a mobile phone by all means, but don't assume you can rely on it in an emergency, since some parts of the moors and hills will not pick up a signal. (If you can make a call and are in a real emergency situation, ring 999 – it is the police who co-ordinate mountain and moorland rescues.)

If this all sounds off-putting, that is certainly not the intention. The guiding principle behind the access legislation is that walkers will exercise their new-won rights with responsibility. Taking appropriate safety precautions is simply one aspect of acting responsibly.

## Access land – what you can and can't do

The countryside which is covered by access legislation includes mountain, moor, heath, downland and common land. After the passing of the Countryside and Rights of Way Act 2000, a lengthy mapping process was undertaken, culminating in the production of 'conclusive' maps which identify land which is open for access. These maps (although not intended as guides for walking) can be accessed via the Internet, at www.countrysideaccess.gov.uk. Ordnance Survey maps

Note: Each walk has been graded, on a scale of ⚘ to ⚘ ⚘ ⚘ ⚘ ⚘ , for the degree of difficulty involved. In general, walks are judged more difficult if they are (a) longer in mileage, and/or (b) involve more rough walking (across open moorland rather than on established footpaths), and/or (c) pose more navigational problems or venture into very unfrequented areas. But bear in mind that all the walks in this book require map-reading competence and some experience of hill walking.

published from 2004 onwards also show access land.

You can walk, run, birdwatch and climb on access land, although there is no right to camp or to bathe in streams or lakes (or, of course, to drive vehicles). The regulations sensibly insist that dogs, where permitted, are on leads near livestock and during the bird-nesting season (1 March–31 July). However, grouse moors have the right to ban dogs altogether, and in some of the area covered by this book this is the case.

Access legislation also does not include the right to ride horses or bikes, though in some areas there may be pre-existing agreements that allow this. More information is available on the website given above and, at the time of writing, there is also an advice line on 0845 100 3298.

The access legislation allows for some open country to be permanently excluded from the right to roam. 'Excepted' land includes military land, quarries and areas close to buildings, and

Penyghent in winter

in addition landowners can apply for other open land to be excluded.

To the best of the authors' knowledge, all the walks in the Freedom to Roam series are either on legal rights of way or across access land included in the official 'conclusive' maps. However, you are asked to bear in mind that the books have been produced right at the start of the new access arrangements, before walkers have begun to walk the hills regularly and before any teething problems on the ground have been ironed out. As access becomes better established, it may be that minor changes to the routes suggested in these books will become appropriate or necessary. You are asked to remember that we are encouraging you to be flexible in the way you use the guides.

Walkers in open country also need to be aware that landowners have a further right to suspend or restrict access to their land for up to twenty-eight days a year. (In such cases of temporary closure there is normally still access on public holidays and on most weekends.) Notice of closure needs to be given in advance and the plan is that this information should be readily available to walkers, it is hoped at local information centres and libraries and also on the countryside access website and at popular entry points to access land. This sort of set-up has generally worked well in Scotland, where arrangements have been made to ensure that walkers in areas where deer hunting takes place can find out when and where hunting is happening.

Walkers will understand the sense in briefly closing small areas of open countryside when, for example, shooting is in progress (grouse shooting begins on 12 August) or when heather burning is taking place in spring. Once again, however, it is too early in the implementation of the access legislation to know how easily walkers in England and Wales will be able to find out about these temporary access closures. It is also too early to know whether landowners will attempt to abuse this power.

In some circumstances, additional restrictions on access can be introduced – for example, on the grounds of nature or heritage conservation, following the advice of English Nature or English Heritage.

Bear these points in mind, but enjoy your walking in the knowledge that any access restrictions should be the exception and not the norm. If you find access unexpectedly denied while walking in the areas suggested in this book, please accept the restrictions and follow the advice you are given. However, if you feel that access was wrongly denied, please report your experience to the countryside service of the local authority (or national park authority, in national park areas) and to the Ramblers' Association.

Finally, there may be occasions when you choose voluntarily not to exercise your freedom to roam. For example, many of the upland moors featured in these books are the homes of ground-nesting birds such as grouse, curlew, lapwing and pipit, who will be nesting in spring and early summer. During this time, many people will decide to leave the birds in peace and find other places to walk. Rest assured that you will know if you are approaching an important nesting area – birds are good at telling you that they would like you to go away.

## Celebrating the open countryside

Despite these necessary caveats, the message from this series is, we hope, clear. Make the most of the new legal rights we have been given – and enjoy your walking.

*Andrew Bibby*

Ingleborough from Widdale

# Introduction

Within the Yorkshire Dales National Park, the Countryside and Rights of Way Act 2000 has increased the area of open access land from just 4 to over 60 per cent of the park. The majority of the walks in this book take advantage of this newly accessible land, and many, especially in the Three Peaks area, are groundbreaking routes over moorland previously forbidden to us. Even in the Howgill Fells (much of which was common land and therefore historically open to roam), the suggested walks turn their back on the well-worn and obvious paths. Instead, they strike out across open moors and fells, following watercourses (and in some cases fording them) to discover landscapes few have experienced.

The Three Peaks of Ingleborough, Whernside and Penyghent all feature in this book, as does The Calf, the highest summit of the Howgills. However, this book is entitled *The Three Peaks and the Howgill Fells* for reasons of brevity only; in fact, it covers so much more. Walks start from Stainforth in the south and from near Newbiggin on Lune in the north; there is also the chance to discover Barbon High Fell to the west and Garsdale in the east. But wherever the routes lead, there is always mountainous landscape to inspire and excite, to reach deep into the soul and lift us up to higher ground.

The environment will often be one of solitary wilderness, where the ability to rely on map and compass is an important criterion. This is especially so in the Howgills, where poor visibility may cause confusion as there are scant navigational clues. Orientation is made difficult by both the close similarity of one rounded summit to the next and a lack of walls above the intake boundaries (where land 'taken in' for cultivation and improved grazing meets the rough moorland beyond).

There are moors with grouse, sparrowhawk and buzzard, as

well as wetlands and flushes with curlew and oystercatcher. There are clear streams and becks that splash down off the slopes, become noisy waterfalls as they gain momentum in deep clefts and join forces to advance as rivers through the dales. There is always interest underfoot, be it peat bogs, limestone pavement, heather, rushes, springy moss, ferns, wild thyme, or grasses bleached to pale cream by the sun.

The fells are home to different varieties of sheep including Swaledale, Rough Fell, Herdswick and Dalesbred; the breed depending on the type of ground and the grass and herbage available. The Howgills are also home to free-roaming fell ponies, in piebald shades of brown and cream. These small, docile creatures graze contentedly as the breeze ruffles their long manes and tails.

Somewhere in most scenes will be man-made structures, such as the field barns which are inevitably scattered about the pastures. Used as storage for fodder, these small, simple buildings provide nesting places for owls and house martins. There are many signs of habitation: secluded farmhouses, open to the upland elements, as well as stone-built village communities that nestle in the shelter of the dales. In Garsdale and Mallerstang the communities are dispersed and strung out along the valley, whereas in Clapham and Stainforth the cottages cluster around the church and green. The site and shape of the villages is often directly linked to the historical period during which people first moved into the area, coupled with the availability of water, the condition of the soil and the ease with which settlements could be defended.

Previous settlers left us more than just the structure of the villages. The Romans bequeathed a tapestry of roads and garrisons, the Scandinavians embroidered our language with place names such as -thwaite (meaning a clearing) and -thorpe (meaning a village or hamlet), and the Normans built us solid, square-towered churches.

Although there are numerous similarities between the Three Peaks and the Howgills, there are also significant differences, especially in geological structure and age. Dividing the two areas is the Dent Fault, a fracture of the earth's crust that was caused when land masses collided about 250 million years ago. Running north-east, the fault links to the Craven Fault (see page 36) near Ingleton and to the Pennine Fault near Kirkby Stephen. The rock structure to the north-west of the fault, in the Howgills area, dates to the Silurian Age 425 million years ago. To the south-east, however, the lower rock of the Three Peaks is predominantly Great Scar limestone of the Carboniferous Age, 340 million years old, topped with Yoredale Series shales and a layer of millstone grit.

In the nineteenth century, Adam Sedgwick was the first to discover this major fault line and to interpret the dramatic events leading to its creation. He was born in the parsonage at Dent and, after attending university at Cambridge, he went on to become Professor of Geology there in 1818. His work in explaining the previously unexplored geology of this part of the country was of considerable importance, and his pioneering research into the older rock systems of Britain laid the foundation for modern geology.

The Dent Fault runs up Barbondale to cross Dentdale and Garsdale, continuing on the lower slopes of Baugh Fell. Garsdale Foot is a particularly good place to observe it, as a section of its route along the banks of the Clough has been designated the Sedgwick Geological Trail, opened in 1985 to commemorate the bicentenary of Adam Sedgwick's birth. The exposed rocks of different ages, laid down over a period spanning millions of years, and evidence of the movement that buckled and fractured them can clearly be seen. It's usual across the Dales for the beds of limestone to be virtually horizontal, but here they have been lifted up and crumbled against the older Silurian rocks. The difference in the age of the rocks either side of the Dent Fault makes the Three Peaks younger than the Howgills by some 85 million years.

The Three Peaks dominate a landscape of grey-white Carboniferous limestone, with fissured outcrops, soaring cliffs and fractured pavements that give the impression of a land whose skeleton is near the skin. This is an area where gills run off the gritstone to meet porous limestone and disappear underground, creating dry, narrow gorges like Trow Gill, potholes such as Alum and Jingle, and caves like Great Douk and Yordas. Gaping Gill, possibly the most famous cave of all, has a main chamber the size of York Minster (see page 46). Victoria Cave, above Settle, is a significant archaeological and geological site where excavation towards the surface unearthed neolithic and Romano-British remains. At a lower level, beneath a layer of clay deposited at the end of the last Ice Age, the bones of large mammals including bear, hyena, lion and hippopotamus were discovered.

Guardians of the Craven Dales, the Three Peaks stand in isolation, their distinctive shapes annexed by broad valleys littered with drumlins (formations of alluvia deposited by glacial floe). Ingleborough, with its level top covering some 15 acres, was once thought to be the highest summit in England. The hill's unique outline is enhanced and enlarged by its buttresses: Simon Fell and Park Fell. Penyghent, seeming out of place with its Welsh-sounding name (a reminder that the Celts settled here around 500 BC), probably means the 'hill of the winds'. Its stepped sides typify the layering of the Yoredale Series of limestone and shale. Whernside's structure of millstone grit is the reason for its name: gritstone quarried from the hill was made into querns (simple hand-mills used for grinding corn). Whernside, therefore, means the hillside where millstones, or querns, came from. But curiously none of the three actually has a *peak*: Ingleborough is flat, Whernside is a ridge and Penyghent a straggle of layers.

▶ page 24

Wild Boar Fell

Each hill has its own identity and, to some degree, climate, but collectively they're almost too famous and well trodden for their own good. Walking, running or even cycling the Three Peaks has become an institution. The first recorded Three Peaks Challenge took place in July 1887 when two masters from Giggleswick School, J.R. Wynne-Edwards and D.R. Smith, walked the 26 miles (42 kilometres) of the course in just over ten hours. The challenge was set, and now individuals and fund-raising groups swarm up and down in increasing numbers.

By contrast, the Howgill Fells huddle together in one rounded, upland mass. To be among them is to be surrounded by them as they hug close like huge, camouflage-coloured velvet cushions. Admired by many travelling the M6 past their western fringes, yet visited by few, the Howgills remain as secretive and secluded as hidden treasure. There's every chance that you won't see any other walkers in a day's hike – but those who don't come this way don't know what they're missing. The smooth roundness of the Howgills reveals minimal erosion by ice floes and the only visible sign of glacial movement is at Cautley Crags, where high, virtually upright cliffs tower above the Spout, a series of waterfalls that cascade downhill for 600 feet (200 metres).

The Howgill Fells take their name from a small settlement in the Lune valley where a number of homesteads, a woollen mill employing up to a hundred workers and a church once thrived. Sadly, the Howgill of today consists of just one farm. *Howe* is a Middle English word deriving from the Norse for hill, so Howgill means a hill ravine. Sedbergh, not Howgill, is the main town of these fells, however. Norse influence is again strong: the town's name derives from the Old Norse word *setbeg*, meaning a flat-topped hill. This obviously doesn't refer to the rounded domes of the Howgills to the north, but rather to the sprawl of Baugh Fell to the east.

Sedbergh, a market town with narrow streets and charming historic buildings, is overlooked by the grassy remains of a motte-and-bailey castle, and encircled by hills and dales. Sedbergh School, a co-educational boarding school, is proud of its many ex-pupils who have gone on to make their mark in the fields of sport, media, arts and science. It was founded as a small chantry school in 1525 by Roger Lupton of Howgill, who was Canon of Windsor and Provost of Eton.

The Howgill Fells massif is surrounded on all sides by the beautiful winding rivers of the Lune, Dee, Rawthey and Clough. Their wooded valleys provide a sheltered environment for a variety of flora, and encompass some of the most scenic and interesting features of the area, such as Swarth Greaves Beck as it cuts its dramatic chasm between Brant Fell and Arant Haw, or the tree-lined Clough river as it meanders through Garsdale. All four rivers converge near Sedbergh and, as Adam Sedgwick put it, 'as the Lune, they make their final escape into Lancashire'.

To the east of the Howgills is the wild landscape of Mallerstang Dale, also featured in this book (Walk 10), with the shapely silhouette of Wild Boar Fell. Just beneath Hugh Seat to the eastern side of Mallerstang valley is the source of the River Eden. The sixteenth-century historian William Camden once described the Eden as 'the most noble river in the county'.

On the Eden's journey north through Mallerstang, it passes Pendragon Castle, one of the homes of Lady Anne Clifford who, in the seventeenth century, engaged in a lengthy legal and political battle for her inheritance, the landholdings of the Clifford estate. Lady Anne travelled extensively through the area between her various castle homes at Skipton, Appleby and Brougham, restoring them after the troubled times of the English Civil War. When Pendragon was rebuilt, Lady Anne had an inscription placed above the main gate. It read: 'This Pendragon Castle was repayred by the Lady Anne Clifford in the year 1660 so as she came to lye in it herself for a little while in October 1661; after it had layen ruinous without timber or any covering ever since the year 1541. God's name be praised.'

The banks of the River Eden have been designated a Site of Special Scientific Interest, but incredibly this is the only formal protection currently given to the northern Howgills and to Mallerstang Dale. For there's a line marching straight across the summit of The Calf, cutting the Howgill range in two. This line is the current northern boundary of the Yorkshire Dales National Park, which takes the course of the pre-1974 boundary line between Westmorland and the West Riding of Yorkshire. Boundaries, admittedly, have to be drawn somewhere but the question must be raised as to why half a mountain range was deemed worthy of being included in a national park, but the other half wasn't.

Fortunately, as this book is being written, proposals are in place to amend the boundaries to reflect the need to protect these natural areas. Following extensive consultation and discussion involving the Friends of the Lake District, the Yorkshire Dales Society and the Ramblers' Association, proposals have been put to the Countryside Agency calling for major changes to the boundaries of the Yorkshire Dales and Lake District national parks. The Countryside Agency has recommended that the northern Howgills and Mallerstang, as well as fells at Middleton, Barbon and Leck, all become part of the Yorkshire Dales National Park. If good sense continues to be shown, the two halves of the Howgills may soon be rejoined, with the whole of this wonderful area benefiting from the protection of national park status. Something to celebrate indeed.

Words can paint pictures of mountains, but, however inspiring and illuminating they are, the pictures remain only in the mind. To really discover these hills, it's necessary to walk them. We've now been given new opportunities to explore the countryside, to view the mountains from unprecedented angles. But new rights bring new obligations. It's up to us all, therefore, to take care not to destroy what we've come to see, and to respect and preserve – as well as enjoy – the land and its flora and fauna.

Ingleborough from Twisleton

# WALK 1

## SMEARSETT AND POT SCAR

**DIFFICULTY** 🥾 🥾 **DISTANCE 5 miles (8 km)**

STAINFORTH — SMEARSETT SCAR — POT SCAR — FEIZOR — HARGREAVES BARN — STAINFORTH

**MAP** OS Explorer OL2, Yorkshire Dales (Southern and Western Areas) and OL41, Forest of Bowland. Alternatively, Harveys Dales West.

**STARTING POINT** Stainforth village (GR 822674)

**PUBLIC TRANSPORT** Buses from Settle to Horton in Ribblesdale stop at Stainforth.

**PARKING** In the national park car park in Stainforth

---

**A fairly easy half-day's ridge walk giving super views of Penyghent and Ingleborough, and across the Ribble valley to Pendle Hill.**

▶ Leave Stainforth by heading north on the B6479, turning quickly left to cross the Ribble and walk up past Knight Stainforth Hall.

■ Monks from Sawley Abbey in Lancashire developed Stainforth (or Stainforth under Bargh, to give it its old name) and, prior to the Dissolution of the Monasteries, the village boasted two windmills and two watermills. The 'stony ford' that connected Stainforth to Little Stainforth (also known as Knight Stainforth) just across the River Ribble was often impassable due to flooding, so the benevolent owner of Knight Stainforth Hall, the Quaker Samuel Watson, had the attractive high-arched packhorse bridge built in the 1670s. The bridge was given to the National Trust in 1931. Just downstream from the bridge is Stainforth Force, the only significant waterfall along the Ribble. Here, the river drops over limestone steps into a wide, deep pool. It's only a short detour from the bridge and is especially worth the effort if the river is high.

▶ Walk straight over the minor road and follow tractor markings uphill, bearing right across two fields to reach a stile on the left of the path ❶. Cross this, then follow the right angle of the wall on the right to another stile that gives access to Smearsett Scar. Keeping the wall on the right, head uphill for approximately 250 yards (250 m) to strike steeply up to the left and reach the trig point on the summit ❷. The hilltop affords distant views to Penyghent, Ingleborough and across to Pendle Hill in Lancashire.

■ Rising to 1832 ft (557 m), Pendle Hill offers a spectacular view over the Ribble valley to the north and Lancashire's cotton towns of Padiham and Burnley to the south. It was on the top of Pendle Hill, in 1652, that George Fox had the vision of enlightenment that led to him founding the Quaker movement.

▶ Head north-north-west along Pot Scar ridge (a faint path can occasionally be found) before reaching and crossing a wall stile ❸. The village of Feizor nestles below, to the left.

■ Although nothing more than a handful of grey stone cottages clustering around a rare and elaborate village water pump, Feizor is a hidden gem. Literally hidden, for high, thrusting scars to one side and rising meadowland to the other mean that one has to negotiate the very last bend down the twisting single-track lane before the huddle of cottages is revealed. The approach road all but ceases soon after it fords a small beck just beyond Old Hall, continuing as an unsealed track beside Feizor Wood.

Old Hall is one of Feizor's oldest dwellings, showing the date 1699 above its door. In his delightful booklet, *Gleanings from an Old-world Hamlet*, Frederick Riley tells of how a small circular gun hole is reputed to be cut in the masonry of the porch, in a direct line with the road leading to the house. As for Feizor's unusual name, Riley explains that there are no fewer than twenty-two spelling variations contained in ancient documents, including Feghers, Feysergh, Feisser and Fesar. Spell it how you will, it's still a lovely place.

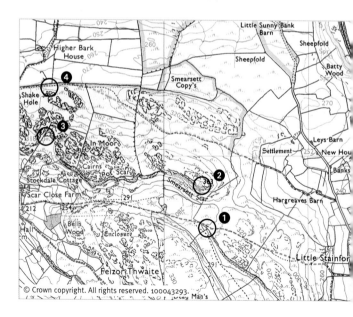

© Crown copyright. All rights reserved. 100043293.

▸ Descend to the right across a grassy dip and find a step stile on the next wall. Now head north across limestone pavements towards Ingleborough, to turn right when you meet a facing wall ❹. A broad grassy path leads the way through a shallow valley on a grand section of walking, before dropping down through the meadows to pass Hargreaves Barn. Turn right on the minor road, heading back to Knight Stainforth Hall and over the river to Stainforth.

■ Just off the A65 between Stainforth and Langcliffe is one of the best-preserved Hoffman kilns in England. This huge kiln, named after its German inventor, was built in 1872 to produce slaked lime (also known as hydrated lime, as it was treated with water). Lime production involved charging part of the kiln with limestone lumps, calcining them and then drawing off the resulting quicklime (burned lime, not yet slaked). The design of the kiln with its twenty-two chambers allowed two continuous firing sequences to take place at once.

The kiln's tall chimney was unfortunately demolished in 1951, but the main structure is in reasonably good condition. The quarry area around the kiln was used for many years as a refuse-disposal site, but the importance of the kiln's heritage has since become better appreciated and the tip has been closed and the site landscaped.

31

# The witches of Austwick

Folklore has it that there are strong links between witchcraft and Pendle Hill in Lancashire. But as the crow flies, or in this case as the witch flew, Pendle isn't very far from the villages closest to the border in Yorkshire. Look westward towards the county boundary from any west Craven high ground and Pendle's distinctive shape is there on the horizon. Lancashire and Yorkshire are divided only by the low-lying land of the Ribble valley – and, after all, witchcraft knew no boundaries! So it's very likely that in the sixteenth and seventeenth centuries the folk on the Yorkshire side, readily influenced by tales of sorcery and mystery, were convinced that broomstick-flying witches with evil on their minds were murmuring through the night sky, crossing the valley, heading in their direction.

Lancashire people reputedly had a variety of methods of placating the black sisterhood; their favourite was to leave a basket of provisions on the doorstep. Yorkshire folk, being true to nature, were a little more thrifty, carrying a piece of rowan wood in a pocket or planting a 'witch elm' in the garden to drive the evil from their land. Horseshoes were nailed to the doors of farm buildings to prevent cattle from coming to harm, and mysterious charms, shaped in a chalk mould, were supposed to give immunity from spells. Nearer the east coast, the custom was to erect weirdly carved 'witch posts' (oak posts often used as a support for the smoke hood above the fireplace) as a protection.

But in Feizor and Austwick, two of the villages closest to that easy flight path over the Ribble from Pendle, another ruse was tried. Protruding slate ledges were built into cottage chimney stacks, to provide flying witches with warm – and external – resting places. Some are two- or even three-tiered, offering enough seating for half a coven. Numerous witches' seats still survive in these two villages.

Dr T.D. Whittaker, writing in his *History of Craven* in 1878, explains why the seats may have been particularly welcome to witches flying over Feizor. 'Of the ten houses in this place, seven are always in the township of Lawkland (near Austwick), within the parish of Clapham; one is always in the Parish of Giggleswick; and the remaining two are one year within Clapham and the next within Giggleswick.' So it is no surprise that the witches were rather bemused when they reached Feizor, and sought some necessary thinking time on the chimney stack seats! And if witches were flying today Feizor would still be confusing them, listed as it is in the Bradford telephone directory but with a Lancaster post code.

The Demdikes of Malkin Tower and the Chattoxes of Higham were the infamous families of the Pendle area who, in the early seventeenth century, were charged with witchcraft and taken to Lancaster Castle for trial. Their confessions resulted in the hanging of eight women and two men in August 1612. But it seems likely that these so-called witches were just very poor folk with mental or physical disabilities, innocent victims of the witch hunt that searched out and publicly exposed those suspected of disloyalty to the State.

Winskill Stones, near Settle

# When the earth moved

If you've ever driven along the A65 between Settle and Ingleton and wondered why the landscape is so different from one side of the road to the other, it's because the road follows virtually the same course as the Craven Fault. This separates the flat-lying Carboniferous limestone rocks of the Dales from the crumpled strata of the Craven plains; the result is that the rich green fields of the Dales limestone uplands halt abruptly and give way to the coarse grass and sedges of the gentler millstone grit country to the south of the road. The movement that caused this cracking of the earth's crust first occurred over 250 million years ago, at the time of the last big movement of land in Britain. (Very slight shifts do still occur, as in the 1946 Skipton tremor.)

The Craven Fault wouldn't have been formed in isolation; instead, a number of faults of different sizes would have occurred in different places at a similar time. Land masses moving against each other would have built up pressure beneath the surface until eventually the rock gave way, shattering and cracking along the fault line. When the movement was strong enough, there would be more than one surface crack and in some cases parallel faults occurred, the rocks behaving like slices of a loaf of bread sliding up and down against each other.

This is what happened to a section of the Craven Fault; between Ingleton (near where the fault abuts the Dent Fault) and Austwick, the Craven is a double fault in two parallel lines. It can be traced along the River Twiss (it is part of the Waterfalls Walk above Ingleton), where the deep valley suddenly changes direction and an almost vertical wall of limestone appears on the thrown-down side of the fault. The two lines run together as far as Austwick, where they separate to become the North Craven Fault and the South Craven Fault. A third split then takes place near Settle, where the Mid Craven Fault turns east.

From Austwick, the line of the North Craven Fault runs via Wharfe through the valley near Foredale Quarry at Helwith Bridge; it can be followed eastwards across the Dales, skirting the foot of Great Whernside, and on to Grassington and beyond. From Settle, the Mid Craven Fault heads past Castlebergh and Upper Settle, then continues through the bumpy Warrendale Knotts and Attermire Scar outcrops (bumpy because made of coral reef limestone instead of the usual Carboniferous stone), on its way to Malham Cove.

The South Craven Fault is at its most obvious along Giggleswick Scar on Buck Haw Brow towards Settle. In his pamphlet *Geology of the Yorkshire Dales National Park*, Dr A.A. Wilson describes Giggleswick Scar as 'a celebrated fault line escarpment. The fault line separates the Great Scar limestone on the left from the millstone grit on the right. The displacement on this fault is locally over half a mile vertically.' Continuing down the valley, the South Craven Fault passes through Long Preston and Hellifield and carries on towards Skipton.

The Dent and Craven Faults create obvious natural boundaries to the west and south of the Yorkshire Dales National Park, and together they form the major geological features of the region.

# WALK 2

## THWAITE AND NORBER

**DIFFICULTY** 👢 👢  **DISTANCE 6 miles (9.6 km)**

| CLAPHAM | TROW GILL | THWAITE | NORBER | AUSTWICK | CLAPHAM |

**MAP** OS Explorer OL2, Yorkshire Dales (Southern and Western Areas) or Harveys Dales West

**STARTING POINT** Old Reading Room (the old national park centre) in Clapham village (GR 745693)

**PUBLIC TRANSPORT** Buses run to Clapham from Horton in Ribblesdale, Ingleton, Settle, Skipton and Bentham. Trains run to Clapham station (approximately 1¼ miles/2 km from the village) from Leeds and Lancaster.

**PARKING** In the national park car park in Clapham

A fairly easy walk that explores varied scenery: bubbling Clapham Beck, the now legally accessible moor over Thwaite and the geologically important Erratics on Norber.

▶ Walk north through Clapham, passing Ingleborough Hall on the right.

■ Ingleborough Hall was built in 1820 as the home of the Farrer family. Reginald John Farrer, a gifted botanist, gardener, writer and painter, was the family's most famous member. He was born with a harelip that required surgical treatment and, although he later grew a bushy moustache to hide the scars, he remained as a consequence shy and solitary throughout his short life.

After attending Balliol College in Oxford, Reginald became a self-taught botanist, rock gardener and passionate plant hunter, travelling extensively to the high-altitude regions of Europe and Asia to collect specimens. In all, he introduced over one hundred new species to this country. Reginald was the author of several botanical books in which he described the new species he'd discovered in colourful prose. His most authoritative title was *The English Rock Garden* which was published in 1919, a year before he died at the age of just forty in Upper Burma. Ingleborough Hall is used today as an outdoor education centre, and part of the garden that Reginald so loved is now Clapham's car park.

▶ Continue past the waterfall and the church before turning left on to Old Road.

■ The waterfall was given 'royal approval' by HRH The Prince of Wales when he visited Clapham in spring 2005. Until local residents became involved in a conservation project to restore the site, the extremely picturesque archway from which Clapham Beck cascades was hidden from view by a wilderness of shrubs and trees. The overgrowth was cleared away, a stepped path built down to the beck and a viewing platform for wheelchair users constructed. The site was then replanted with slow-growing saplings and wild flowers. Funding for the project came from the Yorkshire Dales Millennium Trust, of which Prince Charles is patron.

▶ At this point ❶, take either the free footpath north up Clapdale or the track that passes the lake (subject to a charge of 50 pence).

■ The Farrer family dammed the southern end of Clapdale

in the 1830s, altering the valley and creating the lake. Further alterations then took place when Reginald Farrer turned the high cliffs above the lake into a natural-looking rock garden. Among the rockery he planted bamboo and alpine shrubs, as well as a variety of rhododendrons which blossom in early summer into riotous shades of red.

▶ Whichever route you take, they merge before the entrance to Ingleborough Cave.

■ The dry section of Ingleborough Cave has been open to the public as a show cave for over a hundred years. Since the cave was first explored in 1837, underground labyrinths have been discovered that link it with Clapham Beck Head, another cave very close by that extends northwards below Trow Gill for over 1¼ miles (2 km). Clapham Beck Head is the point where the beck reappears after its subterranean journey

through the innermost part of Ingleborough Cave.

Knowledgeable cavers long held the belief that the beck actually ran from Gaping Gill 1½ miles (2.5 km) away (see page 46), and various potholing clubs and speleological societies carried out explorations throughout the last century to try to prove this theory. Working from both Ingleborough Cave and Gaping Gill, cavers and divers made a little more progress with each trip until, in 1982, it was discovered that the two cave systems came within a horizontal distance of 4 ft (1 m) of each other. After digging out the intervening boulder choke, the first exchange was made between the two caves in 1983. A specialist film crew was on hand to record the event as two cave divers made the journey, one in each direction. They emerged safely to a well-deserved champagne reception.

▶ Just south of Trow Gill (a narrow, dry gorge cut at the end

of the last Ice Age by melting ice running off Ingleborough, which is well worth a diversion), you will meet a wall ❷. Head east here and join Long Lane as it crosses grassy moorland to a gate giving access to the open land at Thwaite. Take a south-south-east direction up and across the moor to reach a large, pointed cairn – and a spectacular view.

Reduce altitude in a southerly direction (there are numerous sheep tracks to help) to meet a ladder stile ❸ giving access to Norber and its Erratics.

■ At the southern end of Crummack Dale, the Norber Erratics are dark boulders of Silurian rock that were torn from the Ribble valley by the melting ice of the Pleistocene period and deposited on this limestone plateau. The boulders have sheltered and protected the soluble limestone on which they sit from the weather, whereas, all around, it has gradually been eroded. The result is that the boulders, some weighing several tons, now sit proudly on pedestals up to 15 ft (4.5 m) tall.

▶ Follow the path through the Erratics to cross the wall ❹ and take the ledge under some attractive Scots pines along Nappa Scars.

■ The cliff face at Nappa Scars shows a cross-section through a series of rocks, telling an interesting geological story. Limestone, at the top, is the youngest layer, below which is a pebbly bed of conglomerates that marks the remains of a whole series of rocks (in this case, Devonian) that have in the past been almost entirely removed by erosion. Beneath the conglomerates are the older Silurian rocks.

▶ Continue along Norber Brow to meet Crummack Lane, and head downhill towards Austwick.

■ Austwick has superbly decorated lintel stones above the doors to some of its seventeenth-century cottages. The village is colloquially known as 'Cuckoo Town'. According to local legend, village folk realized that fortune and weather both improved annually when the cuckoo arrived, and one year decided to try to extend the good times. They found the tree in which the cuckoo perched and laboured all day to build a wall around it. Unfortunately, as it grew dark, and just before the last course was completed, the cuckoo flew away. But the folklore remains, and to celebrate the story Austwick traditionally holds a festival in late May when the village is decorated with cuckoos.

▶ There is a choice of routes back to Clapham: along the higher Thwaite Lane track or a lower alternative on the footpath through the meadows.

■ It was in a small room in Harry Scott's cottage in Clapham that the *Dalesman*, first published in April 1939, had its humble beginnings. Bought by lovers of the

Dales and delivered to Yorkshire expatriates in over fifty countries, today the *Dalesman* has a circulation of just below 44,000, making it the country's biggest-selling regional magazine and one of the great successes of journalism.

Office space was acquired in Clapham after the magazine outgrew its founder's cottage,

and now it is published in the more spacious surroundings of the converted watermill at Broughton Hall near Skipton. Since Harry, there have only been three other editors:

Bill Mitchell, who received the MBE for his services to journalism, David Joy and the present incumbent, Terry Fletcher.

Norber Erratics, Crummack Dale

# Gaping Gill

Numerous infant watercourses begin life on the slopes of Ingleborough and merge to become Fell Beck, which is just another mountain stream until it dramatically throws itself over the edge of a shaft and disappears deep into the ground. That shaft is Gaping Gill, one of the most famous potholes in Britain. This is how Bruce Bedford introduces Gaping Gill in his 1985 book *Underground Britain*:

> The story of Gaping Gill is one which cavers have been reading avidly for the whole of this century, and in the best tradition, it has teased out its surprises and revelations all the way through. Even cavers who have yet to visit Gaping Gill will refer to it in near reverential terms, for they know that this – the grandfather of British caves – is a magnificent and complex system of great variety. Even if Gaping Gill had been discovered only recently it would still stand as one of our greatest caves. But an added degree of importance is imparted by the fact that its first descent marked the birth of serious organized caving in Britain.

When Fell Beck falls down the Main Shaft at Gaping Gill, it does so for 360 feet (110 metres), making it one of the highest waterfalls in Britain. Eventually it hits the floor of the enormous cavern known as the Main Chamber, which has been hollowed out by the power of the cascading water. The difference in temperature between the warm surface air and the cooler air in the shaft produces an atmospheric mist, which appears truly magical when the beck is in flood and water hurtles down flinging spray in all directions. Then, the column of daylight filtering down the shaft plays with the gushing water to make a million droplets of water shimmer, swirled by gusty draughts.

John Birkbeck, from Settle, made the first attempt to descend Gaping Gill's Main Shaft in 1842. He diverted Fell Beck away from the shaft before being lowered on a rope by local farm labourers for 190 feet (58 metres), reaching the ledge that's now known as Birkbeck's Ledge. Alfred Ernest Clibborn was the next to try, in 1882, but he also got no further than the ledge. It was in 1895 that the first successful descent took place, when the experienced French caver, Edouard Alfred Martel, took twenty-three minutes using wood and rope ladders to descend the depths to the Main Chamber.

Martel's descent was heralded a triumph, and organized caving took a huge leap forward. Within a year, Englishman Edward Calvert had also set foot in the Main Chamber, pushing the boundaries further by descending on a seat lowered by a rope and windlass. Today, it is a refined version of this technique that makes it possible for cavers and other visitors to be lowered into the chasm of Gaping Gill with relative ease and speed. For a fortnight each year, two Yorkshire caving clubs organize winch meets at Gaping Gill. An electrically powered bosun's chair, pulled clear of much of the waterfall by a fixed guidewire, lowers people into the Main Chamber, 'like some aerial flyer in an exotic pantomime', as Bruce Bedford describes it.

Excavations to unfold the cave's complex maze of passageways have been gradually unfolding affairs. At the start of the twentieth century, 1 mile (1.6 kilometres) of the system had been investigated, by the middle of the century that figure had reached almost 3 miles (5 kilometres) and today it totals 7 miles (11 kilometres). The passages have proved to be low tunnels of different ages set at varying levels, with rock, mud or boulder floors. Stalagmites and stalactites found to the south of the passages are described as exquisite, and a further five entrances have also been discovered.

As well as passages, Gaping Gill also has a number of large caverns. The most stunning is the Main Chamber, with its dense blue-white micritic limestone and its airy dimensions of 480 feet (145 metres) by 80 feet (25 metres). Near the Main Shaft, where water spray causes erosion when Fell Beck is in flood, the roof reaches its maximum height of 115 feet (35 metres). The floor of the chamber, a fairly level mix of boulders and sand, is normally dry but under flood conditions a lake 20 feet (6 metres) deep can form.

Mud Hall is the appropriate name for a chamber with a copious coating of mud covering floor and walls. Not much smaller than the Main Chamber, the exact dimensions of Mud Hall are difficult to ascertain due to lack of daylight and a partially dividing ridge. There is also Sand Cavern, which consists of two distinct parts yet is usually classed as one large chamber.

Gradually, over the years, knowledge of this fascinating subterranean labyrinth is being pushed forward. But for those who themselves are reluctant to plumb the depths of Gaping Gill, Edouard Martel was considerate enough to leave a record of the delights to be found there:

There is the feeble light of day which, filtering through the spray with millions of prisms formed by the drops, does not seem like anything upon which human eye has gazed. It affords one the impressive attraction of something never seen before. It is one of the most extraordinary spectacles it has been my pleasure to witness.

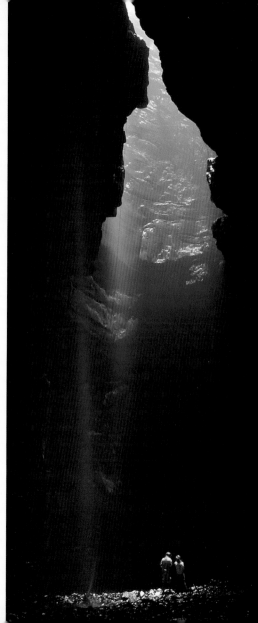

# WALK 3

## CRUMMACK DALE AND MOUGHTON

**DIFFICULTY** 👢 👢 👢 👢   **DISTANCE 7¾ miles (12.5 km)**

HORTON IN RIBBLESDALE — SULBER NICK — CRUMMACK DALE — WASH DUB — MOUGHTON SCARS — MOUGHTON — HORTON IN RIBBLESDALE

**MAP** OS Explorer OL2, Yorkshire Dales (Southern and Western Areas) or Harveys Dales West

**STARTING POINT** Horton in Ribblesdale station (GR 804727)

**PUBLIC TRANSPORT** Trains to Horton in Ribblesdale run from Leeds and Carlisle. There are also buses from Settle, Ingleton, Richmond and Skipton.

**PARKING** In the national park car park in Horton in Ribblesdale

---

Airy and virtually treeless, Crummack is one of the lesser-known small dales and makes an interesting contrast with the lunar-type landscape of Moughton. Parts of Moughton are covered in exposed limestone, some quite crumbly, so progress can be slow.

▶ Cross the railway line at Horton in Ribblesdale station and head north-west uphill on the well-trodden path, passing Horton Quarry with its turquoise lake to the left.

■ Limestone and slate are quarried between Horton and Helwith Bridge as a consequence of earth movements along the Craven Fault, in which the underlying rock was pushed up and exposed (see page 36). Thick flags quarried here were traditionally used for cottage floors and roofs, as well as for tombstones, but the slate quarried today is crushed into chippings for road construction.

▶ Continue through the fields, crossing the tarmac driveway to Beecroft Hall.

■ Beecroft Hall was the chief seat of a manor in Elizabethan times and consisted at that time of some twenty homesteads. More recently, in the 1940s, when the government began to enforce tuberculin testing of herds of milking cattle, the cows at Beecroft were the first in the area to be certified. Soon afterwards Joe Barker took over the Hall and the herd, building up a milk round that was to eventually supply almost all the homes in Horton in Ribblesdale.

▶ Swing uphill across exposed limestone and continue in the same direction up Sulber Nick. Turn left ❶ to Thieves Moss and head on down the gully to Beggar's Stile. Then walk over the wide grassland of upper Crummack Dale to pass to the right of the sheltering of trees at Crummack Farm. Continue on the track to fork left ❷ and follow a walled track down to the Wash Dub.

■ The Wash Dub is the traditional name given to the pen where local farmers and shepherds held their sheep in readiness for washing. In late spring and autumn the beck was dammed to create a pool and the flocks were washed to remove parasites. As the information board beside the pen explains, 'It must have been a cold, wet experience for all concerned.'

▶ Almost immediately after the Wash Dub, take a hard left turn ❸ past Hunterstye and carry on up to the limestone pavements where the land levels at Moughton Scars ❹. Now head south-south-east over the juniper-strewn pavements
▶ page 54

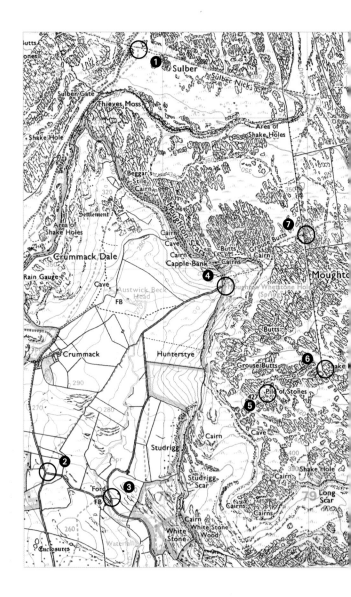

of Moughton, to reach the trig point **5**.

From the trig point, work your way north-east to meet a wall coming in on the right **6**. Keeping to the left of the wall, use it as a guide to head north. Cross the wall at a step stile **7** and then, keeping the wall on your left, walk north to reach another stile. Follow the footpath as it bears north-east between limestone outcrops, then rejoin the path and retrace your steps back to Horton.

■ Penyghent Café in Horton has been run by the Bayes family for forty years and is pivotal to the Three Peaks Challenge. Before setting off, walkers clock in with a card containing their details, so the Bayeses know who they are and which route they're taking. They then return to clock out when the walk has been completed; regardless of how long it takes, a family member will wait up to serve food and drink if required. The record is held by a university lecturer who didn't return until 4.30 am – and Peter Bayes waited up all that time to see him safely returned. The lecturer went off without saying much but returns regularly, each time enthusing loudly to all present, 'This is the only place in the world where they stay up till 4.30 in the morning to serve you tea!'

Wash Dub, Crummack Dale

# Juniper

Juniper is possibly best known as the main ingredient of gin (and is forever linked with the name Jennifer following Donovan's pop song of the sixties). Yet juniper (*Juniperus communis*) is remarkable for more than that. As Britain's only native evergreen shrub, it's so adaptable that it has sixty or so species, contains a magical sap that allows it to thrive at very high altitude and has all kinds of useful medicinal properties.

Juniper forests once covered a large area of the stony uplands of northern England but, largely due to over-grazing, the shrub barely clings to existence in these areas now. Fortunately, action to halt the decline is underway in at least a couple of locations. The juniper on the summit of Moughton (Walk 3) is at the highest altitude recorded for this plant in England, surviving the cold winters through a form of anti-freeze in its sap. To try to help the juniper spread, the farmers who have grazing rights on the fell have agreed to reduce considerably the number of sheep on Moughton in summer and to remove them completely in winter. In the Lake District, juniper has been given its own Biodiversity Action Plan, with the aim of expanding the shrub's diminishing area of cover. Members of the mountain rescue team based at Kendal have helped the national park carry out the experimental planting of juniper on crags and ledges that are beyond the reach of the park's huge sheep population.

Juniper is a variable and highly adaptable plant, ranging from the dwarf form found here in the north through bigger, bushier trees that subsist on the chalk downs of southern England, to numerous developed ornamental varieties. The dwarf shrub bears sharp, well-spaced needles in whorls of three. Its male and female reproductive structures are usually borne on separate plants; the female flowers are tiny green cones that ripen to fleshy, blue-black berries, often with a greyish covering of wax.

It's the juniper fruit, or berry, that's used for flavouring alcoholic beverages, including, of course, gin, named after *Juniperus* through the French, *genièvre*. The berries, which have a fragrant, spicy aroma and a slightly bittersweet flavour, are also used as seasoning in sauces and stuffings, in pickling meats and as flavouring in liqueurs and bitters. Juniper wood was once burnt to produce charcoal for gunpowder, while oil distilled from the wood and leaves of several species is used today in perfumes. Juniper extract is a constituent of diuretic medicines, as well as being added to homeopathic remedies where its soothing and invigorating qualities have proved effective in improving blood circulation, alleviating rheumatism and arthritis, relaxing tense and tired muscles and even ameliorating the effects of colds and 'flu.

Juniper

Penyghent from Silverdale Road

# WALK 4

## PLOVER HILL AND PENYGHENT

**DIFFICULTY** 🥾 🥾 🥾 **DISTANCE 7 miles (11.3 km)**

SILVERDALE    BLISHMIRE HOUSE    CROOKE    PLOVER HILL    PENYGHENT    DALE HEAD    SILVERDALE

**MAP** OS Explorer OL2, Yorkshire Dales (Southern and Western Areas) or Harveys Dales West

**STARTING POINT** Dale Head on Silverdale Road (GR 844715)

**PUBLIC TRANSPORT** Buses from Settle to Horton in Ribblesdale stop at Helwith Bridge. From here a walk of 2½ miles (4 km) up Long Lane to Churn Mill Hole would enable the walk to be started at point **❼**.

**PARKING** Concessionary parking available at Dale Head

A walk on now legally accessible moorland that, despite some boggy sections, offers a fine circumnavigation of Penyghent. A statutory dog-exclusion order is in force across all the access land through which this walk passes.

■ The road from Stainforth up Silverdale has the spacious feel of a wild mountain pass as it proceeds between Penyghent and Fountains Fell, before making its steep descent to Halton Gill in Littondale. Evidence of Silverdale's importance in the time of the monasteries can be seen at Dale Head where, beside the road, the base section of Ulfkil Cross marks the boundary between the abbey estates of Sawley and Fountains. This point is also the boundary of the ancient parish of Giggleswick. Several green lanes converge near by – Dawson Close heading east and Long Lane coming up from Helwith Bridge – which made it a popular meeting point for packmen. The whitewashed buildings at Dale Head were once a packhorse inn; today they are regularly used as a foreground feature in paintings and photographs of Penyghent.

▶ Walk up Silverdale Road past Rainscar and take the gate ❶ on the left, just prior to a cattle grid sign. Turn right and walk along the edge of the meadow, then drop down as the footpath leading to Blishmire House (which is only a barn) becomes clear. Follow the footpath as it crosses a wall and bears right to meet a farm track. Take the track left and use its culvert to cross a watercourse. (This short link on

to access land has been made available through an agreement between the national park and the landowner, at the instigation of the author.)

Cross a stile leading over a fence and head uphill with a wall on your left. Ford Penyghent Gill and continue up the wall as it doglegs ❷. A faint path can be found to the edge of the managed moorland. After another stile, ford Crooke Gill to reach the broken wall around Crooke ❸. Follow the farm vehicle track that keeps close to the inside of the broken wall as it gains height.

When the solid wall descending from the ridge comes into view to the left, cross the broken wall and head up to find a stile at a slight bend ❹, and carry on up to a gate giving access to the ridge footpath. Once across the wall and on the public footpath along the ridge, turn right and enjoy the elevated walk up to the summit of Plover Hill.

■ The wide valley down to the left is the site of another important packhorse way. In *A Picturesque Tour in Yorkshire and Derbyshire*, written in

1805, Edward Dayes describes a journey here: 'From Horton, I immediately entered on the moors, where all is dreary, wild and solitary.' Today, the packhorse route is surfaced as far as High Birkwith, a popular caving spot (perhaps it was Dayes who named the hill immediately north of High Birkwith as Dismal Hill!). It then continues as a stony track over Ling Gill Bridge before climbing open moorland to join the Roman Cam High Road at Cam End. To the south, the route would have linked with Silverdale via Long Lane and Helwith Bridge.

▶ Turn back when you meet a wall ❺. After crossing the stile at GR 840744, strike right across the moorland to pick up the Pennine Way at a junction of paths ❻.

■ Looking north from here towards Penyghent Side there is a good view of The Needle. This little-known feature is a pinnacle of limestone some 60 ft (18 m) high, which stands proud of the adjacent cliffs.

▶ Head south up to the trig point and the curvy new sheltered seating on Penyghent.

■ Over the years, the word Penyghent has been written in many different ways. In 1577, Christopher Saxton (the father of English cartography) spelt it Pennygent. In 1724, Daniel Defoe called it Penigent Hill. In 1810, John Bigland referred to it as Pennygant – but just two years later, in his *History and Antiquities of Craven*, Dr Thomas Whittaker named it Penigent.

Wainwright didn't approve of the Ordnance Survey's hyphenation, or the fact they referred to it as 'Hill'. In *On the Pennine Way*, he bemoans that 'hyphens here, as elsewhere, are an irritation, right or wrong, and modern usage omits them . . . and to add the suffix HILL detracts from a fine name and is never used in conversation. Walkers speak of Penyghent, never of Pen-y-Ghent Hill.'

And today, computer spellcheckers try to change it

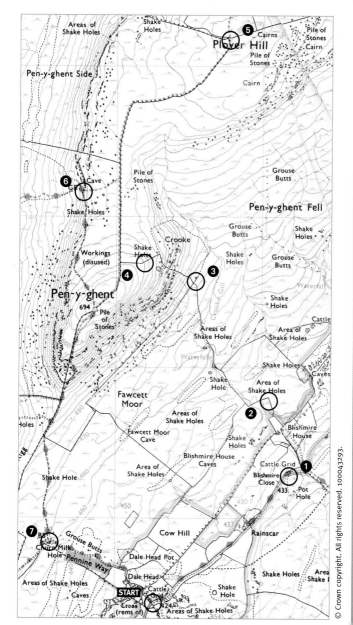

Areas of
Shake Holes

Shake
Holes

**5**

Plover Hill

Cairns

Pile of
Stones
Cairn

Pile of
Stones

Pen-y-ghent Side

Cairn

Grouse
Butts

Pen-y-ghent Fell

**6** Cave

Pile of
Stones

Grouse
Butts

Shake
Holes

Shake Holes

Crooke

Shake
Holes

Grouse
Butts

Workings
(disused)

**4**

Shake
Holes

**3**

Shake
Holes

Pen-y-ghent

694

Pile of
Stones

Areas of
Shake Holes

Crooke Gill

Shake
Holes

Waterfall

Cattle

Waterfalls

Area of
Shake Holes

Shake Holes

Caves

Shake
Hole

Area of
Shake Holes

**2**

Holes

Fawcett
Moor

Areas of
Shake Holes

Blishmire
House

Shake Hole

Fawcett Moor
Cave

Fawcett Moor

Shake
Holes

Blishmire House
Caves

Area of
Shake Holes

**1**

Cattle Grid

Blishmire
Close

433

Pot
Hole

430

437

Rainscar

**7** B
Churn Milk
Hole

Grouse Butts

Pennine Way

Cow Hill

Dale Head Pot

Dale Head

Shake Holes

Area
Shake H

Shake Hole Caves

Areas of Shake Holes

**START**

Cattle
Grid

424

Cross
(rems of)

Areas of Shake Holes

63

to 'penitent' – so you pay your 'Penny' and take your choice!

▶ Descend the steep end (signposted Dale Head), which needs care and probably a bit of scrambling, and continue on the Pennine Way

past the impressive Churn Mill Hole ❼.

■ The Pennine Way was Britain's first national trail and is probably our best-known long distance walk. Running for 270 miles (435 km) from Edale in the Peak

District to Kirk Yetholm on the Scottish borders, the Pennine Way's highest point is Cross Fell in Cumbria at 2930 ft (893 m). Offering the ultimate long-distance walking challenge, the route has attracted thousands of walkers over its forty-year history. Around 150,000 people annually use the trail for day trips and longer walks, with approximately 3,500 a year completing it from start to finish.

▶ Walk through Dale Head Farm back to Silverdale Road.

Limestone pavements and Penyghent from Silverdale Road

# The green man of the quarry

Ingleborough National Nature Reserve has been presented with a new challenge. The reserve, managed by English Nature, is a designated Site of Special Scientific Interest renowned for its wildlife and geology. Already extending to more than 2500 acres, it was handed the additional 100 acres of Ribblehead Quarry when Hanson Aggregates signed a conservation agreement with English Nature in 2000. The old quarry was an inhospitable place: tons of rubble and rock piled among large concrete buildings, and steep cliffs rising above a floor of solid rock. With hardly a veneer of vegetation, it was a scarred, shattered landscape.

Small-scale limestone quarrying has taken place in the Dales for centuries, but the proximity of the Ribblehead site to the railway resulted in commercial extraction on a somewhat larger scale. Opened in 1943 and closed fifteen years later, the quarry was a barren blot on the countryside during the long years before English Nature. Of the 200 reserves in their care, this was English Nature's first abandoned quarry. Hanson moved their heavy machinery back in for a couple of months to demolish the buildings and, under the guidance of English Nature, to construct ponds, boulder fields and marsh areas. Their aim was to create something ripe for natural and diverse recolonization, with hope for the future.

It wouldn't be unfair to say that bare rock and boulders still dominate, but nature's green man is on his way. Helped by the experimental spreading of wood chippings to accelerate growth, vegetation is slowly covering the quarry floor, and the indigenous saplings of alder, birch and willow planted by the stream are beginning to peep over their protective cages.

A nature trail has been created leading up around the top of the cliff and on to the meadows and limestone pavements. Where the soil is shallow, germination will take a while longer yet and a mound of boulders about 50 feet (15 metres) high will probably germinate last of all. 'It's just a pile of stone at the moment but eventually it'll grass over and look like a little hill,' site assistant

Bird's-eye primrose

manager John Osborne explains. 'Then a variety of hardier plants and shrubs that prefer to grow on rocky ground will seed and survive up there. Time will tell, we can only wait and see. Although it's a giant rockery just now, you'd be amazed at what will be here in ten years' time. We'll help where we can, but it's really down to nature.'

Birds, mammals and flowers are all recolonizing. Lapwing, oystercatcher and redshank are building their vulnerable, shallow nests on the ground close to the wet areas, while kestrels and ravens nest more safely in cracks along the cliff face. Delicate pink bird's-eye primroses, yellow and white ox-eye daisies and orchids blooming on stems over 2 feet (nearly 1 metre) tall create a blaze of colour in late springtime. Spiky-flowered sedges and northern spike rush are stunning in the marshy areas, and even in the barren, rocky places there are lizards slinking among the wild thyme. Brown Argus butterflies feed on rockrose, and frogs and toads have found their way to the ponds. Swifts, swallows and house martins have become regular summer visitors, and on warm summer days dragonflies and damselflies dart over the pools.

John is delighted with progress thus far, and is full of optimism for even better things in the future. 'We hope more species of breeding birds will be attracted in greater numbers, especially those that have suffered recently through agricultural changes. We want the place to be as natural as possible so, apart from basic good management, we'll just wait and see what nature brings.'

*Find out more about English Nature's conservation work at Ribblehead Quarry and elsewhere at www.english-nature.org.uk.*

# WALK 5

## PARK FELL, SIMON FELL

## AND INGLEBOROUGH

**DIFFICULTY** 🥾 🥾 🥾 🥾 **DISTANCE 9 miles**

**(14.5 km)**

RIBBLEHEAD   WHIT-A-GREEN   PARK FELL   SIMON FELL   HUMPHREY BOTTOM   SOUTHER SCALES   RIBBLEHEAD

**MAPS** OS Explorer OL2, Yorkshire Dales (Southern and Western Areas) or Harveys Dales West

**STARTING POINT** Junction of B6479 and B6255 at Ribblehead (GR 765793)

**PUBLIC TRANSPORT** Trains to Ribblehead run from Carlisle and Leeds. Buses from Skipton and Richmond stop near the Station Inn, Ribblehead.

**PARKING** There are a number of parking possibilities around the Ribblehead area.

No walking book covering the Three Peaks would be complete without a hike up Ingleborough. Much of this walk is land where, thanks to the Ramblers' Association, the public now has a legal right of access. There are excellent views. Some rough terrain, including possible boggy sections, makes this a challenging walk.

■ Ribblehead, also known as Batty Green, is a turbulent area where winds from varying directions meet in head-on collision, angling the rain horizontally and the winter snows into shapely drifts. It must have provided

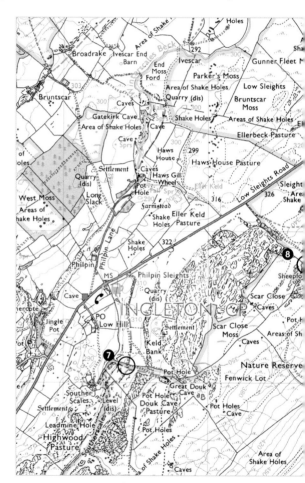

a harsh existence for the two thousand or so contractors, navvies and their families who lived in the extensive shanty town of rough dwellings that covered the area during the construction of Ribblehead Viaduct in

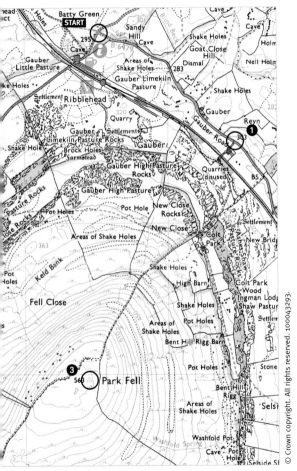

▶ Map continues southwards on pages 72–3

the 1870s. Hardly surprising, then, that more than a hundred workmen died, either through the smallpox epidemic that swept the town or accidents incurred during the difficult and dangerous work. A small memorial tablet in St Leonard's Church at Chapel-le-Dale

commemorates those who died 'on the railway'.

▶ Walk south-east from Ribblehead along Gauber Road (B6479), to turn right ❶ and pass the cottages called Salt Lake. Then bear left just over the railway line on the footpath to Colt Park.

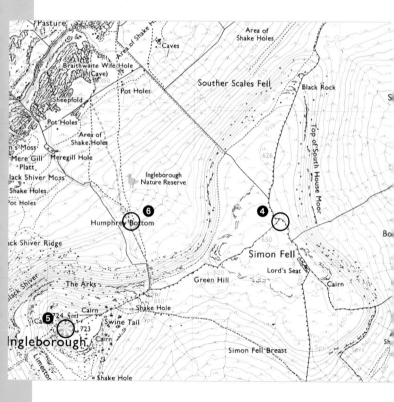

■ The buildings at Colt Park stand on the site of a monastic grange owned by Furness Abbey. The land around them is woodland and meadow, the former being a rare survivor of the type of woods that once covered much of the higher limestone regions. The humidity under the canopy of trees encourages the growth of mosses and ferns, and the colours of summer are added when globeflower, giant bellflower and lily-of-the-valley bloom. As agricultural land, Colt Park meadows were subject to improvement and fertilization before English Nature acquired them. The fenced-off areas are now being used to study the effects of grazing, cutting and fertilizing, in a bid to recreate flower-rich hay meadows. Success is already being demonstrated by the ever-increasing varieties of flowers growing here.

▶ Work your way around the buildings and walk through the narrow meadows towards Selside. At Whit-a-Green Rocks ❷ turn right and head steeply uphill to Park Fell, keeping a wall to your right. When the trig point ❸ comes into view, head for it across the soggy peat bogs, before swinging slightly left to ascend the ridge again, keeping a stone wall to your right.

▶ page 76

Ingleborough from Kingsdale

■ There are superb views here: left across the Ribble valley to Penyghent and right towards Whernside.

▶ Just short of Simon Fell summit, go through a stile at a junction of walls ❹. Initially keeping a wall to your left, proceed over and down to pick up a distinct path and bear left towards Ingleborough summit ❺.

■ The walled shelter on top of Ingleborough was built by Ingleton Fell Rescue Team as a commemorative windbreak in Coronation year, 1953. Other constructions on the summit have been and gone: the earliest is thought to date back to the Iron Age when a hill fort was constructed by the Brigantes tribe. A stone rampart that continued in a circuit for nearly ⅔ mile (1 km) protected a fortified village of at least twenty circular huts. Looking carefully, slight traces of the huts and an inner trench situated just inside the stone rampart can still be identified.

In 1839 a tower was built – and vandalized on the very day it was opened! Hornby Roughsedge, a gentleman from Bentham, purchased the manor of Ingleton and to celebrate his new status had a tower constructed on the highest ground available. At the opening ceremony in summer, Hornby organized races and other sporting events alongside his new creation. He also had food and drink transported to the hilltop. Lots of drink, it would seem, as drunken mayhem broke out, windows and furniture were smashed and considerable damage was done before nightfall.

▶ Keep on up to the summit if you wish, but our route drops down the stone steps at Humphrey Bottom ❻. Enjoy the views across the valley to Whernside. It's not long before you reach flatter walking at Souther Scales, and the limestone pavements and outcrops that are one of the main points of interest during this section of the walk.

Follow the path north for approximately ⅔ mile (1 km). Keeping at the same level, turn right off the main path as it descends to the road **❼**. Proceed through two gates and bear right between the wall and some limestone outcrops to skirt round Great Douk Cave.

■ Great Douk, a fine stream cave, is located in a crater that's about 100 ft (30 m) deep and lined with ash trees. Almost vertical walls drop to the cave's wide mouth, which is overhung with a huge chunk of limestone down which water gushes. To enter, potholers must climb 7 ft (2 m) down a waterfall, which means that they're wet from the start when the stream is high. The bottom of the waterfall gives meandering access to a couple of small chambers and a canyon 10 ft (3 m) high and wide. At one point daylight streams down a vertical shaft from 50 ft (15 m) above, but deep water bars much progress.

▶ Strike left through a small gate and, after bearing briefly right, continue walking through Scar Close.

■ Scar Close is a fascinating area of limestone pavements. The majority of pavements in other parts of the valley have a bare, greyish-white appearance due to over-grazing. In contrast, sheep and cattle have been kept off the pavements at Scar Close since 1980, allowing a diverse and lush woodland to evolve. Under the canopy of small ash, hazel and rowan trees a range of woodland plants bloom, and ferns in particular are abundant. Thin layers of soil have accumulated in the pans (the sunken areas) of the pavements, on which wild angelica and grass of Parnassus grow.

▶ Head north-east with a wall to your right and turn left on a track **❽** just before Fell Close Rocks. Join a footpath to exit on to Low Sleights Road (B6255), turning right to return to Ribblehead.

# The people's folk

Folk songs are the music of the people. Written and sung since time immemorial, traditional songs are passed down from generation to generation. But the repertoire constantly evolves, kept alive and fresh as newly written material is added to the collection, to become the traditional songs of future generations. Whether written about true or imaginary events, to entertain or amuse, folk songs record us – the people – in our everyday lives. They tell of changing occupations such as dry-stone walling, railway building, even knitting (see page 104), or they simply relate what surrounds us – our countryside, towns and villages.

'The Yorkshire Horse Dealers', also known as 'At Clapham Town End', is a traditional song that definitely falls within the amusing category. It tells the story of the implausibly dodgy deal entered into by Tommy Towers and Abey Muggins, a pair of wily horse dealers from Clapham, Yorkshire. They decide to swap horses and, although Tommy's is a poor specimen (all skin and bone), it's an improvement on Abey's – which is dead! Though the story line has local details and is written in colloquial dialect, the song was widely sung throughout the North around the mid-nineteenth century.

A number of songs have been written about the Settle– Carlisle Railway, telling of its wild scenery, superb engineering works and the navvies who built it. Mike Donald, a professional singer-songwriter from Skipton, wrote the best-known tribute:

*In the year of sixty-nine they planned to run a train*
*From Settle to Carlisle, across the mountain range.*
*They employed three thousand navvies to build this*
    *mighty road*
*And across the fells through Appleby that old steam*
    *engine rolled.*

This was the first song Mike Donald wrote about the line. He penned it in 1970, capturing the spirit of the men whose job it was to get 'Up in the mornin', lads, in wind, snow or hail'. A train journey he made from Appleby to Skipton inspired another of his classics, 'Land of the Old and Grey', about economic necessity forcing young people to leave the Dales.

> I am a man of this land
> Thirty long years or more I have worked the Mallerstang Fells,
>    never asked for more.
> Young folks keep moving away,
> Who can get them to stay?
> There's money and there's jobs in the wool towns of
>    the valleys;
> This is the land of the old and grey.

Robert Dugdale, another singer-songwriter, was the vocalist with Farmstead, the Bentham-based folk group who were successful enough in the folk revival days of the 1970s to appear on the *Folk Weave* radio programme and to record an album of songs from Craven. Robert found motivation for his music through his passion for the countryside, and through his concern about its environmental fragility and issues such as quarrying. His composition, 'The Sleeping Lion', became very popular locally. The song is about the familiar landmark of Ingleborough, which he describes as a 'wild and windy mountain', lying proud and mighty like a sleeping lion. The words go on to tell of the variety of people who have made their living under Ingleborough's shadow, the 'coal miners, hill farmers, navvies on the line'. And there's poignancy here, too, as the song recalls all those who've left the Dales behind to seek their livelihoods elsewhere.

Bill Noble, now an octogenarian, played the jug (a musical instrument made from a pitcher) with Farmstead. His jug, over a hundred years old, is a heavy stone one bearing the trademark 'T Brown, Grocer of Clapham'. Bill still plays occasionally at folk nights at the Horse and Farrier in Bentham. He has to – if he's not there the regulars ask, 'Where's jug? Go an' get him!'

Members of a recently formed choir, Settle Voices, are keeping the folk music tradition alive by writing songs about their lives and surroundings. Sue Mackay's words in 'A Picture of Settle' describe the enduring nature of the countryside as well as the bustling feel of the town today:

*Timeless slopes and ancient limestone scars*
*    against the Settle sky.*
*Walls of stone, walls of brick, running roads and rivers flow*
*People live, people work, settled in their lives*
*Monday's children, Tuesday's market, Wednesday's train*
*    comes rattling through*
*With tourists, bikers, cyclists, hikers*
*Settle is alive!*

Another choir member, Pip Grimes, lives in Feizor. The stone walls threading up among the hills and scars around the hamlet provide the inspiration for her 'Dry Stone Wallers Song':

*From the virgin soil we start our toil,*
*The trench is laid and ready.*
*Footings in to underpin*
*And make it good and steady.*
*Facestones, hearting, strength imparting.*

*Throughs to tie each side in.*
*Batter sloping, topped with coping,*
*Work to take a pride in.*

No doubt these recent additions will in time become traditional folk songs that are regularly sung and enjoyed around the Craven area. After all, it was Clapham's Harry Scott, founder of the *Dalesman*, who said, 'Music finds a way to a Yorkshireman's heart.' So, long may our hearts keep the hills (and the Dales) alive with the sound of music – our music.

Clouds come down around Ingleborough

**After fording Kingsdale Beck in the wide, tranquil valley of Kingsdale, this walk takes a route over rough moorland up Whernside (now legally accessible to the public), where it becomes a classic, high-level ridge walk.**

■ Kingsdale stretches for almost 4 miles (6.5 km) to Kingsdale Head and is strikingly flat. Kingsdale Beck often disappears underground, but when it is on the surface it's virtually straight, having been turned into a canal during the eighteenth century. A glacial lake formed here at the end of the last Ice Age. As the glacier retreated, it laid down a huge deposit of silt and grit above Thornton Force at the lower end of the dale, which, for a time, held back the waters of the lake.

▶ From Cluntering Gill Bridge, ford Kingsdale Beck (which may be difficult after a spell of wet weather) and follow the tractor track winding up Long Gill Bank. A wall comes in on the left and the track disappears as the going steepens just prior to reaching the ridge. Follow the wall up, to find a stile giving access to the ridge path ❶. Cross to the well-worn ridge path (part of the Three Peaks route), and head left for a short distance to reach the summit of Whernside at the trig point ❷ (just so you can say you got to the top!).

■ In *Walks in Limestone Country*, Wainwright describes the views from Whernside's summit: 'the panorama is comprehensive, including much of the Dales country and the hills of Lakeland. York Minster has been proved to be in view by an exchange of flashing signals.'

This Whernside, the highest of the Three Peaks at 2419 ft (736 m), isn't the only Whernside in the Dales. Somewhat confusingly, its name is shared with Great Whernside, which is actually 100 ft (30 m) shorter at 2310 ft (704 m), and with Little Whernside at 1984 ft (605 m). Great and Little Whernside rise either side of Angram reservoir, between Coverdale and Nidderdale at the eastern side of the Dales.

▶ Turn back from the trig point and head south along High Pike. Fortunately, the Three Peaks route soon descends, leaving you with the most delightfully quiet ridge footpath, with views right across Kingsdale to Gragareth and left to Ribblehead Viaduct and Ingleborough.

■ As the Settle–Carlisle railway carves its furrow up the Ribble valley, it reaches the line's most imposing feature – Ribblehead Viaduct. The structure is over 100 ft (30 m) at its highest part and more than 1320 ft (400 m) in length. The viaduct's twenty-four arches dominate the

▶ page 90

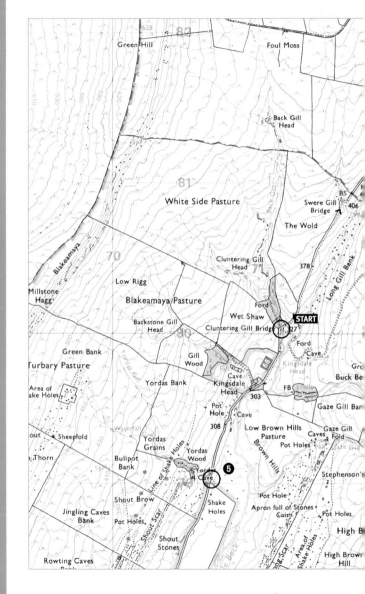

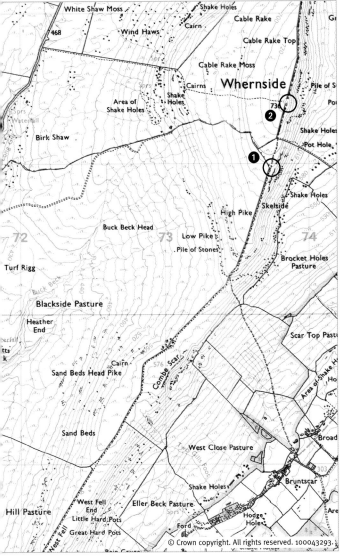

White Shaw Moss

Shake Holes

Cairn

Cable Rake

Cable Rake Top

468

Wind Haws

Cable Rake Moss

Sprs

Cairns

**Whernside**

Pile of S

Area of
Shake Holes

Shake
Holes

736

Po

Sprs

Waterfall

Birk Shaw

2

Shake Holes

Pot Hole

1

Shake Holes

Skelside

High Pike

Buck Beck Head

Low Pike

Pile of Stones

Brocket Holes
Pasture

72

73

74

Turf Rigg

Buck Beck

Blackside Pasture

Heather
End

Scar Top Past

erfa
tts
k

Cairn

Sand Beds Head Pike

Combe Scar

Area of Shake H

Ho

Sand Beds

West Close Pasture

Broad

Bruntscar

303

Shake Holes

Hill Pasture

West Fell
End

Eller Beck Pasture

Little Hard Pots

Sprs

Are

Great Hard Pots

Ford

Hodge
Hole

▶ Map continues southwards on pages 88–9

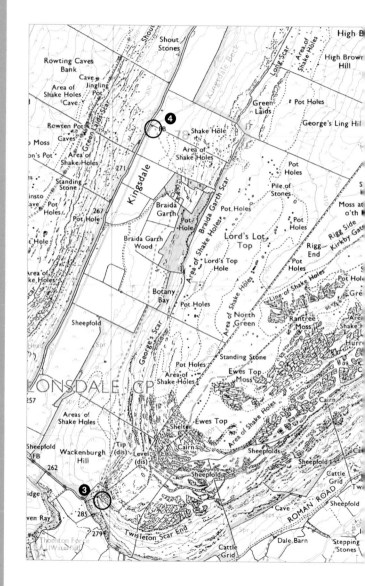

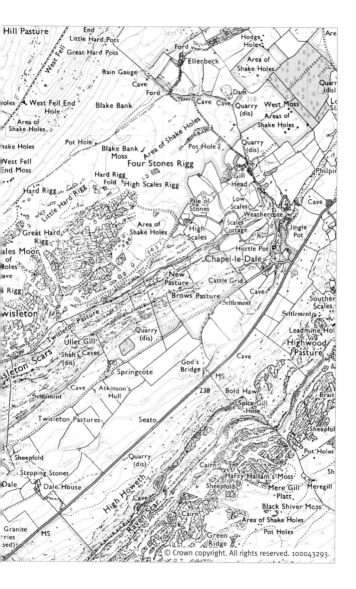

landscape and create a stunning picture when viewed against the backdrop of high fells or, as in this case, from high above. Talking of the viaduct's different perspectives in *Settle & Carlisle Sunset*, P.M. Shaw says, 'It looks impressive as you see it from the train, but the sheer scale of the civil engineering only becomes fully apparent as you stand underneath it. Viewed from the valley floor, it is an awesome feeling to think that it was built by men with virtually no mechanical equipment.'

▶ It's a long straight route down the ridge, but the land undulates interestingly and the elevated views are superb. Drop down the exposed limestone pavements above Twisleton Scar End and briefly join a well-defined path coming in on the left.

■ There's a bird's-eye view from here down the steep-sided valley of the River Twiss, which by this point has absorbed the waters of Kingsdale Beck. The Twiss goes on to join the River Doe just north of Ingleton and become the River Greta, combining to form the main attraction of the ever-popular Ingleton Waterfalls Walk. Thornton Force and Pecca Falls, a little upstream from here, are two of the features along this scenic route, a circuit of 5 miles (8 km) of private land that was first opened to the public in 1885.

The valleys of the two rivers run along the lines of the Craven Fault (see page 36), which has thrown up impressive geological features including the greenish slate rocks of the Ingleton Group, visible beneath the overlying Carboniferous limestone. Ingleton Group slate is over 450 million years old and therefore some of the oldest rock in Yorkshire.

▶ Leave the well-defined path as it swings sharp left ❸ and a step stile gives access to the narrow path along the side of Wackenburgh Hill. Carry on to the farm at Braida Garth, where the route between the farm buildings is signposted.

■ An attic room at Braida Garth was at one time covered with turf and used as a venue for cockfighting. Gamecocks were collected from Ingleton two weeks prior to a fight, to allow time for training and for the birds to be fed on specially nutritious food. W.R. Mitchell, in his book *High Dale Country*, reports that 'There was betting, of course, sometimes £100 a side.'

▶ Walk diagonally across a field to reach a footbridge below the road ❹. Cross the bridge and turn immediately right along the west bank of Kingsdale Beck.

■ The route along Kingsdale Beck, which is often dry in this part of the valley, passes the Apron Full of Stones, a prehistoric ring cairn built almost completely of grit and sandstone.

▶ Exit back on to the lane opposite Yordas Cave ❺.

■ Formerly a Victorian show cave for which permission to visit had to be sought from Braida Garth Farm, Yordas Cave is today open to all. Except for good torches and wellies or boots, Yordas doesn't necessitate specialist caving equipment, although a visit is best avoided during floods when it can be dangerous. The cave is in a very picturesque wooded setting, and the large walk-in entrance is reached down a set of stone steps leading to an obvious low arch. After the arch, the roof is mostly lofty, about 60 ft (18 m) high, but there are dangling rocks. The cave has many natural features, including a waterfall that cascades into a circular cavern known as the Chapter House. Folklore recalls that Yordas was the home of a Nordic giant who hunted for little boys and dined on them in the cave!

▶ Walk north past Kingsdale Head Farm to return to Cluntering Gill Bridge.

Ribblehead Viaduct and Whernside

# On stony ground

The stark beauty of the Craven Dales countryside is dominated by an abundance of grey-white limestone features: high cliffs, dry-stone walls, fractured pavements, deep-delving caves. The distinctive landscape of naturally fissured rocky outcrops is known as 'karst'.

The limestone of Craven consists mostly of recrystallized crushed sea shells and the skeletons of sea creatures. To discover why, we need to go back 350 million years to the beginning of the story, when layers of chalky white mud were laid down in what were then shallow, tropical seas. As the mud changed to limestone it shrank, causing cracks that split the layers from top to bottom, and earth movements have since caused long cracks which run across the limestone north-west to south-east.

Potholes, caves and subterranean streams have formed because limestone, although hard, is the only common rock that is soluble; its purity is such that, as it dissolves away, it leaves little in the way of mud or sand to form soil. Rainwater finds its way down through the cracks and the higher its content of carbon dioxide, the more the limestone dissolves. Then, when water evaporates again inside the caves, lime can be deposited once more as stalactites or stalagmites.

The largest of the pavements can be up to 65 feet (20 metres) deep and cover many acres of land. The process of weathering carves intricate networks of deep channels, giving the separated blocks of limestone, which measure an average of 6½ feet (2 metres) long by 3 feet (1 metre) wide, the misshapen appearance of crazy paving. The indentations on the top surface which retain rainwater are called pans, and the shallow channels draining these are runnels. The deep channels, or joints, are grikes and the blocks of limestone are known as clints.

The warm, humid microclimate of the grikes shelters an array of flora, especially ferns such as maidenhair, spleenwort and rigid buckler fern. Flowering plants flourish too, the most common of which is the tiny-flowered wild thyme. Early purple orchids, yellow rockrose, bird's-foot trefoil and white limestone bedstraw create a colourful palette in early summer, before making way for the blues of midsummer when scabious and harebells bloom.

The limestone pavements are now protected under Annex 1 of the European Union's Habitats Directive and the most important of the pavements have international designation as Special Areas of Conservation. Legal protection is necessary because limestone has been a fashionable horticultural decoration for some two hundred years, and acre after acre of weather-worn limestone pavement has been ripped up to be used in rock gardens or as ornamental walling. Limestone pavement is unique and cannot be replaced.

According to studies published in 1995, there are 6425 acres (an area approximately the size of Harrogate) of limestone pavement throughout Britain, of which it's estimated that less than 3 per cent remains undamaged. Thanks to the efforts of the Limestone Pavement Action Group, this tiny percentage is now protected by British law and should be allowed to survive intact. Under the Wildlife and Countryside Act 1981, the local authority can make a Limestone Pavement Order (LPO) to protect a pavement. Once an LPO is in place, removal of rock becomes a criminal offence, and anyone taking it from a designated site can be prosecuted and fined, even if the rock is loose or lying in a field. LPOs are now in place on all major and most minor areas of limestone pavement, and extraction is illegal throughout Craven.

*The Limestone Pavement Action Group can be contacted via www.limestone-pavements.org.uk.*

# WALK 7

## BARBONDALE, CRAG HILL AND
## BARBON HIGH FELL

**DIFFICULTY** 👢 👢 👢 👢 **DISTANCE 11 miles (18 km)**

HODGE BRIDGE → BARBON → BLINDBECK BRIDGE → LITTLE AYGILL → CRAG HILL → HAZEL SIKE → HODGE BRIDGE

**MAP** OS Explorer OL2, Yorkshire Dales (Southern and Western Areas) or Harveys Dales West

**STARTING POINT** Hodge Bridge on the A683 Kirkby Lonsdale–Sedbergh road (GR 624826)

**PUBLIC TRANSPORT** None available at time of publication

**PARKING** Adjacent to Hodge Bridge

**A walk that keeps to watercourses for the most part, leading on to the fells of Crag Hill and Barbon High Fell, now legally accessible. Some boggy sections, and a little scrambling may be necessary.**

■ Although the OS map indicates that Hodge Bridge is not Roman, the A683 is in fact constructed on the site of a Roman road. Just west of Middleton, 2 miles (3 km) north of here, the remains of a milestone from the period were discovered in 1836. It has since been moved and re-erected on private land.

Leaving the line of the A683 to hug close to the Lune on its south-westerly course, the remains of the Roman road head due south, soon becoming a familiar long, straight line.

To the east of Casterton and Kirkby Lonsdale, Wandales Lane and Long Level still make use of sections of the Roman road. It provided access to the Roman fort on the northern bank of Leck Beck at Over Barrow, 1 mile (1.6 km) to the west of Cowan Bridge.

▶ Walk along the lane beside Barbon Beck, through the village of Barbon.

■ Barbon village is a charming, sleepy backwater of whitewashed and stone cottages. Its name is mentioned in the Domesday Book as Berebrune.

Before closure in 1953, the London North-Western Railway from Ingleton to Tebay ran through the village, but new housing developments make it difficult to find the route of the line now. The church of St Bartholomew was built in the perpendicular style in 1893. The view of the fells from its east windows is so good it would render the lengthiest sermon bearable!

▶ Take the track on the left just past the church and walk up in the direction of Barbon Manor. A footpath sign leads you down to the right at Pencil Brow ❶, on to a linear green lane running through pleasant woodland beside Barbon Beck.

■ Sequestered among the trees, the Italianate Barbon Manor was built by the Kay-Shuttleworth family in Victorian times. If you're puzzled by the strength of the crash barriers erected on a bend partway up the drive, it's because the Westmorland Motor Club uses the locality as the setting for a number of vehicle rallies each summer. Hill races for different types of cars including saloons, sports and rally cars are held in June; the motorcycles, three-wheelers and quad bikes get their turn in July.

The woodland ends and there are now good open

views to the surrounding fells, including Barbon High Fell in front of you.

▶ Cross Barbon Beck at the footbridge and turn right along the lane. Soon after crossing Little Aygill at Blindbeck Bridge, turn left up a stony track. When it bends sharp right, leave the track and bear left to cross the gill near a delightful series of short waterfalls **2**. Continue in a south-easterly

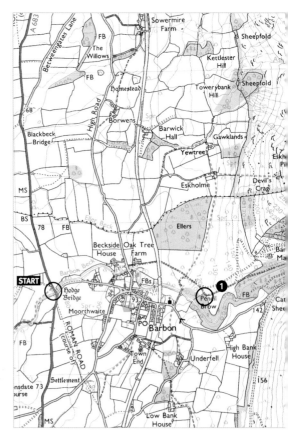

direction up over boggy ground between the gill and a fence. Cross the gill where the fence drops down beside it, and head up to join a footpath and reach a gate ❸.

■ The picture-postcard white cottage ahead is Bullpot, a former farmhouse that's now used as a caving hut. The building gets its name from the nearby Bullpot of the Witches, an impressive cave

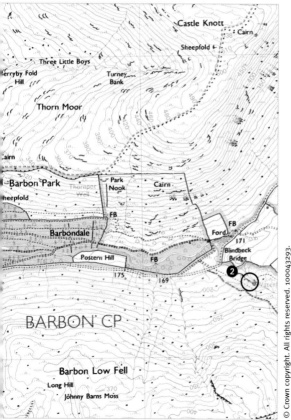

▶ Map continues eastwards on pages 100–101

50 ft (15 m) deep. Bullpot, along with Lancaster Hole, Cow Pot and Leck Beck Head, is part of Ease Gill, one of Britain's largest cave systems with over 30 miles (50 km) of interconnected passageways.

A team from the British Speleological Association discovered the first entrance into the main system at Lancaster Hole in September 1946. Except in times of flood, Leck Beck is

subterranean until it resurfaces at Leck Beck Head, and what the Northern Pennine Club refer to as 'some of the finest caverns in England' are due to the Beck's course of underground meanderings through the limestone. Further downstream, Leck Beck flows beneath the busy A65 at Cowan Bridge on its journey to join the River Lune.

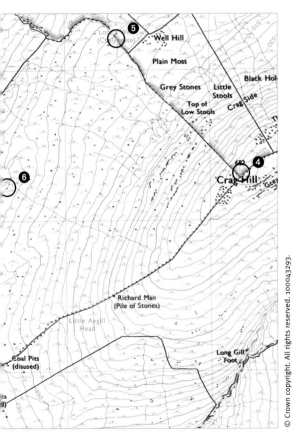

▶ Take the stile beside a gate on the left and follow an easterly course beside Little Aygill. Narrow sheep tracks work along the little valley but some scrambling is necessary.

■ There is a long tradition of coal mining in this region. A number of outlying coalpits were situated close to the watercourses on Barbon High Fell. They are shown on a map dated 1834 and are thought to have been the usual mixture of adits, shafts and bell pits. Barbon and Casterton pits are believed to be the oldest in the area, dating as far back as the reign of Charles I. Coal was still being worked close to the Ease Gill caves up to the mid-1940s.

In his book *Coal Mining in Lunesdale*, Phil Hudson describes a couple of accidents that took place on Barbon. The Kirkby Lonsdale parish register for 1761 records 'the burial of John Frankland, described as a stranger, who was killed by falling into a coal pit near Barbon'. (It's unclear whether he was a miner or not.) Another fatality occurred in 1831 when the *Lancaster Gazette* reported that 'Adam Braithwaite, a collier, had died at Barbon colliery through a fall of the roof'.

▶ Continue uphill, keeping to the left of the gill and a wall, to reach the summit of Crag Hill ❹.

■ There are superb views from here of Dentdale, Whernside and Gragareth, and across the Lune valley to the Langdales and other Lakeland fells.

▶ Turn north-west and descend to the left of a wall past Grey Stones. Turn south-west near Lord's Well ❺ to pick up the left bank of the emerging Hazel Sike ❻. Follow the stream to the stile across the fence and rejoin the main footpath down to Blindbeck Bridge. Retrace your steps through the woods to Barbon and back to the starting point at Hodge Bridge.

Little Aygill, Barbon High Fell

# Knitting in the Dales – Sarah's story

The year is 1785 and Sarah is the youngest inhabitant of High Pasture Farm at Garsdale. This is perhaps how she might tell her story:

We keep our small herd of cows down on the meadows by the river. The land above us is called Baugh Fell; it's boggy moorland with rough grass, but our sheep graze happily there. My grandparents live in a cottage near the river and I walk down to see them every day. They're always knitting, but so are all the people in these dales. Mother and father knit when their other work is done, and my brothers and sister knit as they sing and play. I'm learning to knit too; I go to a knitting school where we also learn some spellings and sing 'knitting tunes'. They're like the nursery rhymes mother used to teach me, and I like them. Our teacher says it's the choruses that are important as they help us pay attention. I've got my own small knitting sheath and needles now, only we call the needles 'wires'. We have nicknames for other things too: a 'clue of garn' is a ball of wool, and as the wool is coarse and sticky, we call it 'bump'. One of my favourite songs goes:

*Bell-wether o' Barking, cries baa, baa,*
*how many sheep have we lost today?*
*Nineteen we have lost, one have we faun'*
*Run Rockie, run Rockie, run, run, run.*

We have to try to knit one round of a stocking in the time it takes to sing that. As we knit more rows, the

Knitting played a crucial role in the economy of the Dales

numbers of the lost sheep go down and the found ones go up. We try to see who can finish a row first; we call that 'strivin' needles'.

When we all knit together at home, mother tells me to 'keep short wires', meaning I've to work as near the needle tips as possible. I'm really happy when we all sit knitting together, the clickety-click of the needles sounding like the beating of a drum. We join in the rhythm by counting our loops like the shepherds count their sheep, 'arn, tarn, tethera . . .'. My brothers and sister knit stockings and caps and earn just threepence for each one. As for mother, she knits so fast her loops fly off the wires quicker than I can see. She's so speedy she can knit a jersey in a day.

Every year, father salves our sheep with a horrible mixture of tar and butter. Then he has to wash it all off before they're clipped. Mother spins some of the wool into yarn for stockings and I love to hear the whirr of the spinning wheel.

When it's getting dark in the evening and us young ones have taken a candle upstairs to bed, father and mother walk with the lantern to a neighbour's house to 'gang a sitting', spend the evening round the fire knitting. My grandparents often go too, and neighbours along the dale. They knit away, singing knitting songs or reciting poems or telling ghostly tales.

Every now and then they come to our farm, and my elder sister, who's learnt her letters better than me, reads a passage from a book. I crept down and peeped through the door once and it was beautiful: them all sitting round, rocking to and fro, knitting by the light of the peat fire; not a sound but the clickety-click of the wires and her voice.

All our knitted things are collected by the stockinger, a man who carries them from the dale in a covered cart to somewhere called Kendal. There's a big market there, but I've never been.

Even though quite poorly paid, knitting played an important part in the economy of the northern Dales for about three hundred years. The most comprehensive account can be found in *The Old Hand-Knitters of the Dales* by Marie Hartley and Joan Ingilby. It was Robert Southey, in his miscellany entitled *The Doctor*, who painted the detailed picture of the knitting industry entitled 'The Terrible Knitters e' Dent'. Even though the phrase has stuck, it's rather ambiguous on two counts: the word terrible was meant as a compliment, and the industry was common to many other areas, including Sedbergh, Mallerstang and the Rawthey valley – and not forgetting, of course, Sarah's Garsdale and the Clough river.

# WALK 8

## GRISEDALE PIKE AND EAST BAUGH FELL

**DIFFICULTY**  **DISTANCE 10½ miles**

**(17 km)**

GARSDALE STATION → GRISEDALE → GRISEDALE PIKE → EAST BAUGH FELL → EAST TARNS → GRISEDALE GILL → GARSDALE STATION

**MAP** OS Explorer OL19, Howgill Fells and Upper Eden Valley, or Harveys Dales West

**STARTING POINT** Garsdale station (GR 788917)

**PUBLIC TRANSPORT** There are trains to Garsdale on the Leeds–Settle–Carlisle line. Buses from Hawes (route 113) stop Monday–Saturday at the railway station, and a solitary Tuesday bus (route 804) currently runs between Sedbergh and Garsdale (details from 01423 526655). Additionally, a shared hire-car service connecting with the station is operated by Clifford Ellis (01969 667598).

**PARKING** Adjacent to the station

The desolation of Baugh Fell is perfect for peaceful walking, but the going is often boggy and rugged and a compass is a necessary companion.

▶ From Garsdale station, cross the A684 and take the path immediately opposite, signposted to Grisedale. A tractor track misleads by going straight up; instead, take the footpath heading off left and cross a wall at another footpath sign. Follow the faint trod over boggy ground, passing the ruin of Blake Mire, to exit on to Grisedale Road by Rowantree Farm **❶**.

■ Grisedale is an isolated upland valley that is geographically an outreach of upper Wensleydale. Sheltered to the north by the dark moors of Aisgill and Wild Boar Fell and to the west by Baugh Fell, Grisedale has a wild and lonely feel to it. 'Grise' comes from the Norse word for pig, and it was Norsemen who first settled in Grisedale, developing farms with names like Round Ing and High Flust.

Sixteen families lived in the dale at the start of the twentieth century. A dame school was built, and a tiny chapel was opened in the late 1880s in memory of Richard Atkinson, an Evangelist who had spiritual influence over the passionate Quakers and Methodists of the Dales. Alcohol was frowned upon: there were six small chapels but not one public house between Grisedale and Sedbergh.

The continuous battle against the harsh elements and infertile land slowly, over the years, reduced the number of inhabited dwellings to one. In recognition of this graveyard of ruined farmhouses, Barry Cockcroft used the term *The Dale that Died* as the title of both his book and the Yorkshire Television documentary he made about Grisedale. But the dale didn't die completely. Although there's only one farmer working the land, a few of the farmhouses have been renovated and are inhabited again, and the little chapel has also been converted to a house. And though there are many sad skeletons, there are also sheep in the fields and flowers in at least some of the gardens. Grisedale may not be as boisterous as it once was, but it's still alive.

▶ Turn right along the lane and then left at Moor Rigg **❷**, on to the footpath beside Grisedale Beck past Reachey and Galey Hill.

■ In August 1889, 4½ in (115 mm) of rain fell in three hours, swelling Grisedale Beck, a tributary of the River Clough, into a torrent and devastating Garsdale. Throughout the valley there was extraordinary flooding,

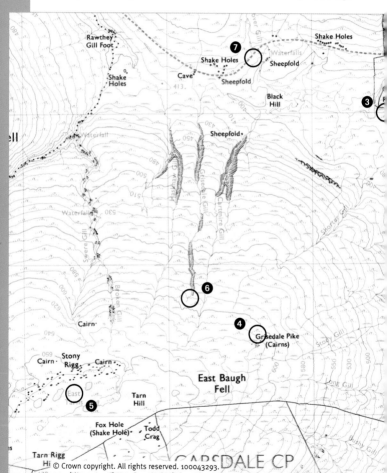

which completely wrecked
three bridges and washed
away footbridges, sections of
road and miles of walls and

fences. Trees were uprooted
and houses filled with sand
and mud. A wave of water
swamped the playground of

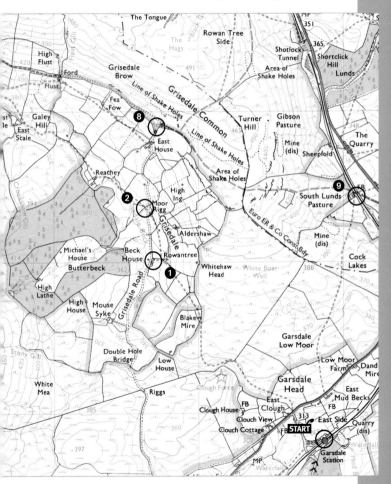

the village school, flooding it to a depth of 5 ft (1.5 m). The weight of water burst open the doors of the school and pushed in the windows. The teacher instructed the frightened children to stand on their desks. As the water was rising towards the children's feet, the men of the village waded in, picked up all the children and carried them out to safety.

▸ Keep Grisedale Beck close to your left until GR 765940 **3**. Ford the beck and, heading south, ascend and pass through a gap in the wall. Proceed through a gate beside a ruined barn to the right, which gives access to the open moor, and keep south across the fell to pick up the watercourse of Shorter Gill.

Follow the gill for a while, but leave it again to reach the cairns on Grisedale Pike **4**. Then walk west-south-west over Tarn Hill, passing a single tarn to reach the numerous larger ones at East Tarns **5**. At GR 743922, head north-east, passing the right-hand one of two cairns on

The Clough from Garsdale Head

Stony Rigg to locate the source of Grisedale Gill ❻ and walk down its left side.

■ The strip of land between Grisedale Gill and Haskhaw Gill is a narrow watershed. To the east, the becks pour into Grisedale and eventually join the Clough in Garsdale. To the west, the streams head down to the Rawthey in Uldale. It's but a brief divide, as all the water flowing off the north of Baugh Fell, whether into the Rawthey or the Clough, meets up again as it joins the River Lune.

▶ Moving north-east, work your way uphill to meet the footpath coming around Holmes Moss Hill ❼ and proceed to join the farm track after the ford at High Flust. Carry straight on as the track becomes surfaced and swings downhill ❽. Gradually leave the wall to the right, heading uphill to a ladder stile, before dropping down the reedy land of South Lunds Pasture to the railway footbridge ❾. Now head south over Garsdale Low Moor to reach Garsdale station.

■ Dandrymire Viaduct carries the Settle–Carlisle line across Garsdale Head on the route from Garsdale station up to Kirkby Stephen. The original plan was to construct an embankment. Two years were spent tipping stone into Dandry Mire to create a solid foundation, but all that happened was that the sides of the mire became distended by as much as 24 yards (22 m) in one direction. So, after a rethink in 1872, a viaduct was proposed. A foundation was secured for the piers by digging down 50 ft (15 m) through soft peat to find the bedrock. The viaduct has twelve arches (the fourth and eighth piers were built more robustly than the others), and is 227 yards (207 m) long.

# Change here for a station with a difference

There's probably not another railway in Britain that has captured people's imagination as the Settle–Carlisle line has done. When it was threatened with closure during the 1980s, the campaign to preserve it mounted by the Ramblers' Association and others led to such publicity that the line is now enjoying quite a renaissance. Upgrading of station infrastructure by the Friends of the Settle–Carlisle Line (a voluntary organization which promotes the railway as part of the national network), as well as track investment of £1.5 million by the operators, have resulted in healthy usage of both freight and passenger services. It's not hard to see why people like this line. The wild beauty of the scenery is window-dressed to perfection as the line passes over elegant viaducts, through mountain tunnels and around ledges cut from the high fells. The sublime engineering is testament to the audacious Victorians who built the route.

Constructed during the 1870s, the Settle–Carlisle line irrevocably altered the landscape and the lives of the people along its route, none more so than at Garsdale. In his book *Garsdale*, W.R. Mitchell describes it as a very special station: 'The only junction on the line, it had a turntable on which locomotives were apt to spin out of control, a tank house also used as a social centre and the highest water troughs in the world . . . t'junction was more than a railway station, it was the pulse of a small community in which stationmaster, signalmen and porters were heroes.'

Garsdale station, or Hawes Junction as it was originally known, spreads high along the open fell, backed by lofty Pennine hills and facing full on a heartless, hurrying wind. The railway's links to Scotland via Carlisle, to Northallerton via Hawes and to Leeds via Settle put Garsdale's once-scattered farming community firmly on the map. The railway provided jobs, and workers from Bedfordshire, Worcestershire and Norfolk found lodgings in the dale or moved into one of the sixteen specially built 'railway servants' cottages'.

Boasting a stationmaster's office, booking hall, porters' room and general and ladies' waiting rooms, the station clattered with the continual movement of passenger and freight traffic. W.R. Mitchell again: 'The trains were so packed wi' folk popping across platforms from one train to another; if you wanted a seat on the Hawes train you couldn't get one – you had to ride in the guard's van.' There were horse-boxes bound for the races at Middleham, cattle wagons bringing Scottish cattle south and milk trains six days a week. Timetable idiosyncrasies were not uncommon: the Leeds train scheduled to leave at 10.22 am always left at 10.15 until after 20 July, when it left at 10.05!

Aisgill, just north of Garsdale and the highest point on any British railway, is the summit of an incline of 22 miles (35.5 kilometres) from the Ribble valley, known as the Long Drag. Generations of perspiring footplatemen, having thrashed their locos up to the top, were so elated to see the distant signal for Aisgill that it became nicknamed the Star of Bethlehem. A tank house holding 80,000 gallons of water was sited at Garsdale so passing engines could be assured of sufficient steam to finish the Long Drag.

Enterprising families of the railway workers and local Dales folk turned the space beneath the tank into a social centre. They laid a wooden floor, stripped red upholstered seating from an old carriage to line the walls, installed two coal-burning stoves and raised funds to buy a gramophone and piano. Dances, concerts and whist drives whiled away winter evenings. Some were rather raucous: 'it was a reight good do – we hed piano ower three times' is one recollection recorded by W.R. Mitchell. The tank house became a regular venue for birthday parties and even weddings. An adjacent supper room was added: an old railway carriage kitted out with stove, boiler, tables and seats. Over a hundred people regularly packed the tank house and supper room, ignoring the rattle of teacups as the expresses thundered by a few yards away. There were no toilets, just 'outside', but they reasoned that the sheep didn't care.

A regular woman passenger from Wensleydale, feeling sorry for the railwaymen living miles from anywhere, donated 150 books to the station. In 1938 the ladies' waiting room on the 'up' platform became the home of the station's library, and stationmaster Ferguson took on the additional role of chief librarian. He must have been proud of this unusual facility, keeping the books, including novels by Dickens, Scott and Verne as well as non-fiction and reference books, spick and span behind glass. During the 1950s the county library service added modern fiction to the collection.

Not wishing to be outdone by the waiting room on the 'up' platform, the waiting room on the 'down' platform became

Garsdale station, as it was in the late 1930s

Garsdale Head's church. The officiating clergyman arrived for the monthly service carrying a small bag holding his communion plate and vestments. A little table was covered with a cloth as a makeshift altar, and hymn books were distributed, as well as prayer books marked 'Hawes Junction Waiting Room Service – not to be taken away'. The services became a feature of local life before the Second World War, with residents subscribing towards the cost of a harmonium; an act they later regretted as it was described as 'an ill wind that nobody blows any good'!

With the exception of Harold Thwaite, who remained in his job as porter until nudging seventy, station employees came and went. One of those who moved on was Signalman Sutton, for it was he who was deemed responsible for the horrific accident that occurred on Christmas Eve 1910 in which twelve passengers died. Traffic on the line was busy that night as strong winds drummed the rain hard against the windows of the signal box. Two engines bound for Carlisle saw an all-clear signal and set off. But the Glasgow express had been given the all-clear, too; it thumped into the back of one of the Carlisle trains, shunting it into the other and derailing all three. Then the high-pressure gas main that lit the express ruptured and exploded in a single, brilliant flash of flame. Signalman Sutton, realizing with horror that he had forgotten about the Carlisle engines, reputedly turned to his relief signalman and said, 'Will you go to Stationmaster Bunce and tell him I'm afraid I've wrecked the Scotch express.'

What of Garsdale station today? Sadly, it is unstaffed and the tank house, as well as much of the junction line to Northallerton, has been dismantled. But it survives. Freight trains pass through, passenger sprinter services still call, and if the Wensleydale Railway Association's campaign to restore the junction line down to Hawes and beyond is successful, Garsdale's golden days may return once more.

# WALK 9

## THE CALF

**DIFFICULTY**  **DISTANCE 8 miles (13 km)**

SEDBERGH — ARANT HAW — THE CALF — BRAM RIGG — SEAT KNOTT — CRAGGSTONE WOOD — SEDBERGH

**MAPS** OS Explorer OL19, Howgill Fells and Upper Eden Valley, or Harveys Howgill Fells Superwalker

**STARTING POINT** Sedbergh Tourist Information Office (GR 659922)

**PUBLIC TRANSPORT** Buses run to Sedbergh from Kirkby Lonsdale, Kendal and Kirkby Stephen (Monday–Saturday), and from Dent station (Wednesdays and Saturdays only).

**PARKING** Various car parks in Sedbergh

**This is a classic high-level walk on and around the Howgill Fells, and a must to see them at their finest. The ascent up Soolbank is steep, but the views are worth the effort.**

■ Sedbergh, the centre of an area of dispersed Norse settlements, is a picturesque town of narrow streets and historic buildings. On the edge of the town at Castlehaw (the steep hill overlooking the confluence of the Rawthey and Lune rivers), the Normans built a motte-and-bailey castle to defend themselves against marauding Scots. They altered the shape of the top of the hill to accommodate the fort, and in times of danger gathered their

119

animals into the bailey and themselves into the motte above. The town was given a charter of markets and fairs in 1251, and a small weekly market is still held.

Sedbergh was brought to the nation's attention in January 2005 in *The Town that Wants a Twin*: a charming twelve-episode BBC2 television documentary telling of the town's twinning escapades. Although delegations were sent from several European towns, the people of Sedbergh voted overwhelmingly in favour of Zreče in Slovenia. With 3000 inhabitants, Zreče is also a rural town set among rolling hills.

▶ Head east along the main street and turn left on the unsealed lane signposted Castlehaw, to pass the grassy elevation where the castle once stood. Cross Settlebeck Gill in Jubilee Wood and keep uphill on the obvious path.

■ Jubilee Wood, a section of Settlebeck Gill, is being

managed to conserve its diverse flora and fauna.
It is a remnant of the type of woodland covering the area long ago, with trees such as oak, ash, sycamore, rowan

and hawthorn. Depending on the season, you may spot wood anemones, bluebells, wood sorrel and primroses, and a wide range of birds from buzzards to blue tits, as well as winter visitors such as redwings and fieldfares. There's evidence of coppicing, the cutting of wood a few feet up the trunk to produce a new growth of

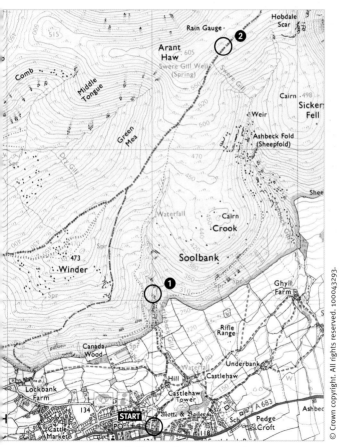

▶ Map continues northwards on pages 122–3

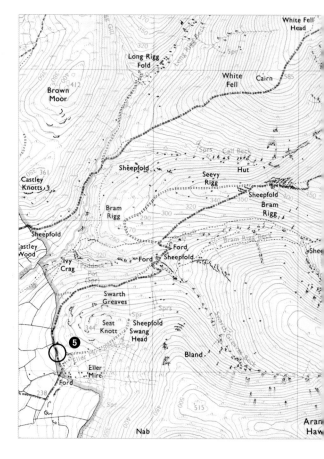

narrow branches suitable for tool handles, fence posts and charcoal. Red squirrels are still seen here (see page 134), and many other mammals, including rabbits, stoats, badgers and foxes, find refuge in heaps of dead wood and under low bushes.

▶ Drop down right to cross the

across the moor, past the source of Settlebeck Gill, and on to the obvious track up Arant Haw. Continue ahead on the same track as it swings right to meet the main, more defined path ❷ up Rowantree Grains.

Follow the path as it swings right, then bear left along a delightful elevated stretch over Bram Rigg Top ❸ and on to the trig point at The Calf ❹.

■ The Calf, or just 'Calf' as the locals refer to it, is the highest of the Howgill Fells and offers spectacular all-round views. From here on a clear day you may see Morecambe Bay, Wensleydale, Malham Moor, Lancaster, Helvellyn and Nine Standards Rigg. This summit is the current northern boundary of the Yorkshire Dales National Park.

▶ Retrace your steps for 300 yds (300 m) and take the narrow path heading south-west down the ridge. Ford Bram Rigg Beck near some old sheepfolds and continue round the contours of Seat Knott ❺.

beck again above a waterfall ❶, and then head up keeping the watercourse to your left. Skirt the lower flanks of Soolbank and rise up the contours (which may mean some scrambling) to head

Cut across Eller Mire to the higher corner of the intake wall and rise up to join a path that you follow south, with lovely views across the emerald fields of the Lune valley. Drop down to ford Crosdale Beck ❻ and go through the first gate on the right to arrive below the bower of beech trees in Craggstone Wood. Keep left, following yellow marker posts down to Howgill Lane and bear left.

■ Howgill Lane is on the site of a Roman road (in fact, the same Roman road that is met at the start of Walk 7). As it comes up from the south, the route of the road crosses the River Rawthey at a deep ford, before passing close to Ingmire Hall and joining Howgill Lane near Height of Winder Farm. The Romans occasionally bent the route as they tried to find the best crossing of the numerous

The Howgill Fells

becks flowing down off the westerly Howgills, but otherwise the road progressed in an almost straight line until it headed west to pass through the Lune Gorge. Appreciating that this corridor had strategic importance, the Romans built a fort at Low Borrowbridge to guard it.

In *Roads and Trackways of the Yorkshire Dales*, Geoffrey Wright describes the section near Carlingill as '18 ft wide with a foundation of large stones, with yellow clay beneath and a closely packed surface layer up to 4 in thick'. Further north, the road would have gone to the Roman fort of Brocavum (Brougham), before ending at the Roman wall at Carlisle.

▶ Take the left fork at the junction and head back down to Sedbergh.

■ The Wilson Run cross-country race takes place at the end of the Lent term at Sedbergh School, upholding a tradition that began in 1881. The steeplechase of 10 miles (16 km) is named in honour of Bernard Wilson, a master at Sedbergh who encouraged scholars to discover the countryside beyond the confines of the town. The course includes the ascent of some of the nearer fells and is so challenging that record-breaking times are rare. However, a new time was set in 1993, when Charles Sykes completed the course in 1 hour 8 minutes 4 seconds. A different sort of record was set in 2001, when female scholars ran the race for the first time. The Wilson Run is now open to all students over sixteen years who wish to partake and who are deemed fit enough by the school doctor. An evening concert is held after the race at which all the pupils who've completed the course are honoured by being called up on to the stage.

# WALK 10

## WILD BOAR FELL

**DIFFICULTY** 🥾 🥾 🥾   **DISTANCE** 6 miles (9.6 km)

| THRANG BRIDGE | HIGH DOLPHINSTY | WILD BOAR FELL | THE NAB | HIGH DOLPHINSTY | THRANG BRIDGE |

**MAPS** OS Explorer OL19, Howgill Fells and Upper Eden Valley, or Harveys Dales West

**STARTING POINT** Thrang Bridge on the B6259 Garsdale–Kirkby Stephen road (GR 783005)

**PUBLIC TRANSPORT** One bus from Kirkby Stephen to Hawes makes the return trip through Mallerstang valley on Tuesdays only (March–October). It passes Thrang Bridge at approximately 11.00 am on its way to Hawes and returns about 4.00 pm.

**PARKING** A small amount of off-road parking is available at Thrang Bridge.

**Wild Boar Fell looks majestic as it rises to its shapely summit above Mallerstang Dale, and just begs to be climbed. This elevated walk lives up to every expectation, with sublime and far-reaching views.**

▶ From Thrang Bridge choose either the lane or one of two footpaths heading south to reach Hazel Gill Farm ❶. Keep uphill left of the farm buildings to cross under the railway line.

■ The route of the railway through Mallerstang valley is typical of the Settle–Carlisle line as it jauntily traverses a ledge cut into the fell side, high above the valley bottom. The train's elevation offers a good view of the dale's farmsteads, strung along close to the valley floor, and the tapestry of walls and fields rising up the opposite side towards Mallerstang Edge. This stretch of the line between Garsdale and Kirkby Stephen, a distance just short of 10 miles (16 km), is the longest without a passenger station. Proposals

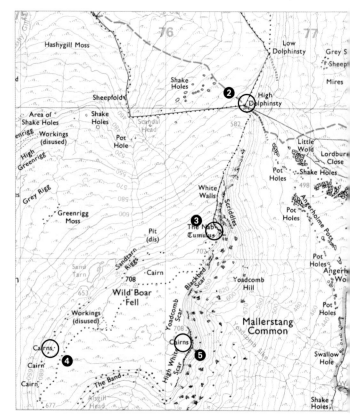

to build one opposite Outhgill were considered, but failed when the money to construct an approach road could not be found.

Just south of Mallerstang, the train crosses Aisgill at the highest altitude throughout the length of the line. A little further north, it passes what remains of Pendragon Castle, bearing the name of legendary Uther Pendragon, father of King Arthur.

▶ Follow the path as it swings up and crosses below the place where tiny Hazel Gill falls down a series of steps. Keeping the watercourse on your left, proceed uphill to the saddle at High Dolphinsty ❷.

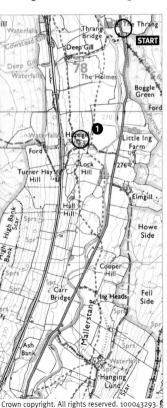

■ As you gain altitude, the line of a walled track rising across the opposite hillside becomes visible. This is the High Way, running south from Thrang Bridge to the A684 at the bottom of Cotterdale. It was the busy main mountain bridleway used by drovers and packhorses, and was also the route that Lady Anne Clifford travelled on her extensive and well-documented journeys in the seventeenth century. Lady Anne was born at Skipton Castle and became High Sheriff of Westmorland. She was the owner of Pendragon, as well as of castles at Appleby, Brougham and other places. The elaborate entourage with which she travelled consisted of nearly three hundred servants, as her favourite bed, bedding, carpets, curtains, food and so on had to be carried too!

Also visible as it breaks the skyline is an object that, from this distance, could easily be mistaken for a large and ancient standing stone. It is in fact *Water Cut*, a thoroughly modern sculpture by Mary Bourne, and one of the ten sculptures placed along the Eden valley that are collectively known as The Eden Benchmarks. Commissioned by East Cumbria Countryside Project to celebrate what they refer to as 'a very special river', *Water Cut* is the sculpture nearest to the source of the River Eden.

▶ Leave the path opposite a gate and follow the faint markings up along the edge to the cairn at The Nab ❸. Turn south-west, following the line of cairns and, just after the third

one ❹, strike east across the extensive summit moorland to meet a fence as it doglegs.

■ The second cairn encompasses Wild Boar Fell's summit trig point at 2324 ft (708 m), although High Seat across the dale is the taller by just a few feet (one metre). A little to the west of the summit of Wild Boar Fell is Sand Tarn, a small stretch of water which gets its name from the powdered millstone grit of the tarn's small beach. Mixed with tar, the grit was used by blacksmiths to hone the blades of their cutting tools.

In his book *Mallerstang Dale*, Dr John Hamilton suggests that Wild Boar Fell is so named because, in the fifteenth century, Sir Richard Musgrave killed here what was thought at the time to be the very last wild boar in England. Dr Hamilton goes on to say, 'When Sir Richard's tomb in Kirkby Stephen church was opened during the restoration of the side chapels in 1847, a boar's tusk was found. So it must be true!'

▶ Bear left at the fence and walk to the beehive-shaped cairns, or riggs ❺.

■ One can't help but wonder why so many cairns have been built in this area. They're all well constructed from limestone blocks, measure up to 10 ft (3 m) high and are usually in the familiar beehive shape. Besides the seven here on The Nab, there's another cluster further north on top of Little Fell, which are smaller versions of the cairns at Nine Standards Rigg. Were they built as markers for shepherds, or to identify routes, or do they stand as memorials or graves? Who knows!

▶ Work your way back along the edge to High Dolphinsty and descend via the same route.

■ Whichever route you take from Hazel Gill Farm, you will cross the River Eden. The source of the river is at Redgill Beck, on the open moorland just beneath Hugh Seat on the opposite side of Mallerstang Dale, at a height of 2200 ft (670 m). The river gains strength as it flows along the valley and through the towns of Kirkby Stephen and Appleby in Westmorland. Slowing to a meander once the gradient levels, the river picks up pace again through the deep sandstone gorges of Penrith before calming once more at Carlisle's wide flood plain. After Carlisle, the Eden joins with other rivers to form the Solway Firth estuary.

The waters of the Eden are home to salmon. In the spawning grounds of the river's upper reaches they lay their eggs in gravel, where the water has plenty of oxygen, and shoals of young fry can be spotted keeping themselves safe in the shadows. It's usually three years before the salmon make their journey out to sea, migrating to their feeding grounds in the North Atlantic. Using their exceptionally strong sense of smell to identify their 'home' river, the Eden, they then return in the autumn to continue the eternal cycle.

Wild Boar Fell

# Red squirrels

The red squirrel is one of Britain's favourite native mammals. Sadly, populations are becoming rarer and rarer. It is small areas of woodland in north Yorkshire and Cumbria that provide a home for some of the last surviving colonies in England.

The decline of the red squirrel began in 1876 when wealthy landowners released a few North American grey squirrels into Britain as a novelty. Little did they realize that the greys compete with reds for food, and also pass on a deadly disease called parapoxvirus to them. Efforts to conserve the red squirrel became increasingly urgent during the latter part of the twentieth century, as the greys became ever more firmly established at the expense of the reds. The decline has been so dramatic that today only 30,000 red squirrels still survive in England, compared to over 2 million greys. In other words, the reds are outnumbered sixty-six to one.

A campaign called Red Alert was set up in 1993 and has since been working hard to ensure the survival of the species. Based at the regional Wildlife Trusts, Red Alert is a partnership between conservation organizations, businesses and a great many volunteers, all of whom are doing their bit for the preservation of the red squirrel.

Red Alert is focusing on a long-term strategy of creating conifer reserves for the red squirrels. Conservationists have discovered that they are very partial to woodland seeds, including the seeds of various conifer cones, as well as hazel and beech nuts. They have to compete with the greys for the hazel and beech nuts, but grey squirrels are not interested in the conifer cones. Conifer plantations were never previously considered advantageous to wildlife but, surprisingly, it seems they can provide red squirrels with a haven for the future.

Red squirrel

So far, a network of twenty red squirrel reserves has been established in conifer forests across northern England, where the woodland is managed specifically to ensure good food and shelter for the reds. For example, it is important to maintain a mixture of trees of different ages to reduce the impact of poor cone-producing years in particular species. The species of conifer preferred by the reds are Scots pine, Corsican pine, Norway spruce and larch.

While they provide food for the reds, large-seeded broad-leaved trees such as oak, elm, sweet chestnut, beech and hazel also attract grey squirrels, so Red Alert is campaigning to stop the planting of certain broadleaf trees within the reserves. By contrast, small-seeded broad-leaved trees such as willow, aspen, birch, alder and rowan are acceptable, since they are not favoured by the greys.

'Although it's widely known that red squirrels have survived in the Cumbrian areas of the national park, there have been reports in recent years of red squirrels in adjacent areas across the county boundary in Yorkshire,' says Ian Court, species officer for the Yorkshire Dales National Park. 'The park authority are working with a number of organizations, local landowners and residents in the Hawes area of the park to determine the status of red squirrels, and the initial results are encouraging and show that there's currently a healthy population of red squirrels in the area. It's hoped that with the continued goodwill and support of local people, forest managers and owners, the woodlands in the area will continue to be managed for the benefit of red squirrels.'

The summer is a lean time for red squirrels, when they have to rely on whatever they can find in the way of flowers, shoots, berries or fungi. Where red squirrels remain, Red Alert encourages people to give them a helping hand with a feeder of high-quality food, placed out of the reach of cats. A leading manufacturer of wild-bird food is currently developing a new 'red-only' feeder which, if successful, may give the reds some of the help they need to survive.

Grey squirrels are being controlled in the 'buffer zones' surrounding each forest refuge after it became clear that action was necessary if the extinction of red squirrels was to be averted. Although the Wildlife Trusts do not undertake the killing of greys lightly, an active trapping campaign is under way, with paid contractors employed and traps supplied to local volunteers.

Volunteers are heavily involved in the work of Red Alert in north-west England. As well as trapping greys, they help by reporting sightings of both types of squirrel. These sightings are collated on a database, making squirrels among the most reported mammals in Britain. Local volunteers also feed reds, count populations and even install aerial rope bridges to reduce squirrel road deaths.

*Red Alert North West can be contacted via www.redsquirrel.org.uk.*

# WALK 11

## WANDALE AND RAVENSTONEDALE

**DIFFICULTY** 👢 👢 **DISTANCE 6½ miles (10.5 km)**

RAWTHEY BRIDGE → MURTHWAITE → HARTER FELL → RAVENSTONE DALE → NARTHWAITE → RAWTHEY BRIDGE

**MAP** OS Explorer OL19, Howgill Fells and Upper Eden Valley, or Harveys Howgill Fells Superwalker

**STARTING POINT** Rawthey Bridge (GR 714979)

**PUBLIC TRANSPORT** Stagecoach route 564 connects Penrith, Kendal, Kirkby Stephen and Dent along the A683. There is a bus stop by the Cross Keys pub and drivers will make request stops at other places (Mondays–Saturdays; telephone 0870 6082608 for times).

**PARKING** In the car park beside Rawthey Bridge

This walk, taking in three farmsteads with 'thwaite' (meaning a clearing) in their name, touches on the wilderness of Ravenstonedale. It can be extended by a further 2½ miles (4 km) to visit Cautley Spout.

▶ Follow the road north-east for ¼ mile (0.4 km) from Rawthey Bridge.

■ While the Swale, Wharfe, Aire and most other Dales rivers run east to the North Sea, the River Rawthey, like the Ribble, flows westwards to the Irish Sea. Rawthey Bridge is situated among delightful fells and spans the river as it flows from the Uldale valley before turning to join the Lune beyond Sedbergh. The current bridge was built in 1822, 80 yards (80 m) from the site of the old one, and has a carved stone head below each parapet.

The road up to Rawthey Bridge from Sedbergh (the A683) became a turnpike in 1765. The turnpike continued north along what is now the minor road past Cold Keld (which was licensed as an alehouse in the mid 1800s) and Foggy Gill.

▶ Cross Sally Beck by the footbridge ❶, signposted to Murthwaite, and follow the path uphill.

■ Only one dwelling exists at Murthwaite today where at one time there used to be four, all with whitewashed frontages that gave the area the nickname 'White City'. Murthwaite Park, an area of broad-leaved woodland, is a designated Site of Special Scientific Interest. The trees shelter numerous damp glades where orchids bloom in early summer. Pied flycatchers and snipe are two of the less common birds that frequent the park.

▶ Keep to the left of the farm and proceed through a gate to take the right-hand option of a choice of tracks. Continue for about 100 yards (100 m) before bearing left at the signpost for Stonely Gill. Soon after a wall comes in on the left, walk uphill ❷ on a defined grassy path as it ascends the contours of Harter Fell and provides elevated views down to Adamthwaite and along Ravenstonedale.

■ Wandale is connected to Ravenstonedale by the narrowest of roads – barely the width of a small car. But for the inhabitants of Adamthwaite, the rambling, seventeenth-century farmhouse set in an isolated hollow at the head of Wandale Beck, this 2½-mile (4-km) wafer of tarmac is a link with the outside world.

▶ page 142

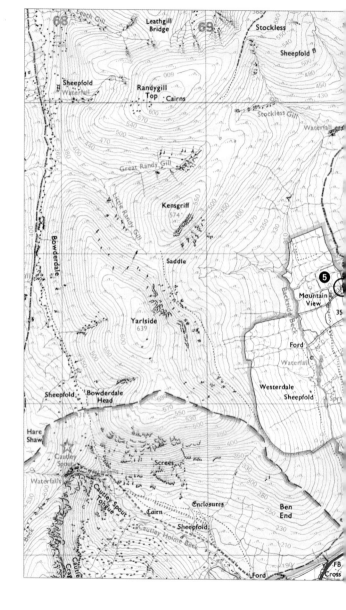

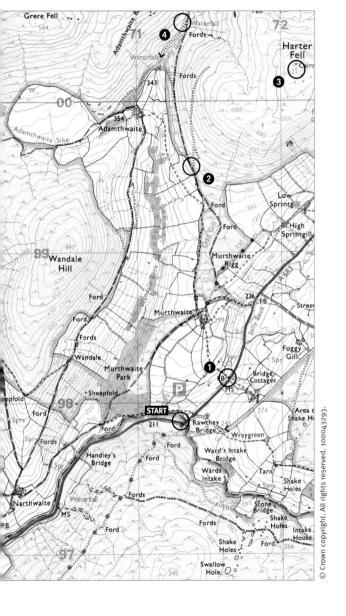

Even though the main road passes within 1¼ miles (2 km) of the house, anyone approaching from the south has to take a long and circuitous route north and then west across to Ravenstonedale village, before heading south down the narrow lane. The alternative, of course, is to walk like us from Rawthey Bridge!

Adamthwaite is the highest farm in the parish. It still retains its spinning gallery, for in the eighteenth and nineteenth centuries agriculture only just exceeded in importance the knitting of woollen stockings and gloves as the main trade throughout Ravenstonedale.

▶ When the track fades, head uphill to reach the cairn on the summit of Harter Fell ❸, from where there are good views east to Stennerskeugh Clouds and Wild Boar Fell. Descend from the cairn to join a watercourse and walk down beside its tiny waterfalls to cross Stonely Gill ❹ and turn left on the road.

■ This is the narrow road leading north up Ravenstonedale to the village of the same name. Reverend William Nicholls wrote in 1850, in his *History and Traditions of Ravenstonedale, Volume II*, that 'The morals of the people are good, and the farmers are thrifty and intelligent.' At one point the village had three grocers, a butcher and slaughterhouse, a joiner, tailor, blacksmith, dressmaker, post office, cobbler, various banks, a set of petrol pumps and a weekly market. Today it has an unspoilt air, with its attractive clusters of stone properties spreading along the roadsides, but not one of those businesses has survived.

One Ravenstonedale business that is still highly successful is the Cumbria Classic Coach Company, which regularly supplies old buses for television programmes such as *Born and Bred* and *Heartbeat*. Their speciality is halfcab

Cautley Spout from the Rawthey valley

coaches, in which the driver's cab is separate and situated in front of the passenger compartment. The oldest bus they own is a 1946 Leyland Tiger.

▶ Turn off the road to the right on the stony track signposted Narthwaite. Follow the obvious track to the right of a modern barn and through a gate. Then bear left towards the wall and an old building, and follow the wall to another gate. This section may well be boggy. Go through the gate to swing in a southerly direction on a barely visible path over moorland terrain.

The path improves as the intake walls come close to the appropriately named Mountain View ❺, and it's a grand walk down to Narthwaite. Work right between the farm buildings and down among trees to ford Backside Beck. Leave the path as it nears the road and cross the footbridge close to the

Cross Keys, to walk back up the road to Rawthey Bridge. Alternatively, extend the walk by ignoring the footbridge for now and continue up the path to visit Cautley Spout.

■ Cautley Crag is a shoulder of The Calf (the highest of the Howgill Fells), and the exception to the Howgills' norm of smooth rounded heights and deep winding streams. The rugged cliffs and corrie of Cautley Crag provide the only notable evidence of glacial erosion in the whole group of hills. The waters of Red Gill Beck cascade down the high, vertical camber in a series of stepped waterfalls known as Cautley Spout.

▶ The footpath, which follows the course of Cautley Holme Beck and heads up Cautley Spout Tongue to the waterfalls, is very steep towards the top.

# From coal to curlew

All is silent now. Once more, only the haunting cries of curlews break the hushed peace of the moors. Gone are the calls of grimy-faced colliers, the scratching of pickaxes and shovels and the rumbling of laden carts. It hardly seems possible in such wilderness, but a few hundred years ago these were the familiar noises of the uplands above the valleys of the Lune, Dee, Rawthey and Clough, when the coal-mining industry was in full swing.

The coal was found in layers just beneath the thin capping of millstone grit and in the sandstone stratum of the Yoredale rocks. Although coal did not provide many colliers with full-time work or make a significant difference to the economy, it lay in sufficient quantities to be comprehensively worked during the peak of mining in the eighteenth and nineteenth centuries.

The majority of mines were at heights of 1000–1500 feet (300–450 metres), in isolated places that lacked easy access. The altitude worked in favour of the carters who delivered the coal to Garsdale, Dent and Sedburgh, as it meant their delivery route was downhill nearly all the way. The numerous sites at which the extensive seams of Garsdale Fell colliery were quarried were linked by narrow green roads to Galloway Gate (which became known as Coal Road), a packhorse thoroughfare from Lancaster to the north. The pits on Casterton Fell were accessed via another ancient way called Turbary Road, so called because the people of Thornton in Lonsdale used it to reach the common land where they had the right to dig peat ('turbary' means both a place where turf or peat is dug and the right to dig). For lengthy journeys, coal was usually carried by pack ponies, but by the end of the eighteenth century small fixed-axle carts called tumbrels were being used for short distances.

Where the coal was in shallow seams, open-cast methods of mining were the norm. Adits, or drift mines, were driven almost horizontally into the hillside, ideally beside a beck or rocky outcrop. It was often the case that seams would be followed uphill; if they deepened or became too difficult to work, the miners, or diggers, would simply give up. The term 'digger', used instead of 'miner' by many of the colliery workers to refer to themselves, is evidence of the shallowness of the mines.

The majority of the coal found in this area was too brittle for the hearth, but it was put to good use to fire lime kilns; the spreading of burnt lime to sweeten rough pastureland was a farming technique used from the mid-eighteenth century to the later nineteenth century. A green track would drop from the upland coalpit to the mid-ground where the limestone was extracted, and continue on down the hill to a simple semi-circular lime kiln, built close to the pastures where the burnt lime was to be spread.

The end of significant coal mining in north-west Yorkshire came around 1840 with the arrival of economically viable methods of transport. The opening of local canals and railways meant that abundant quantities of cheaper, better coal from the deep mines of south Yorkshire became available. One by one, the small mines were abandoned to the elements. The stone structures that had provided shelter for the miners became ruins, and vegetation encircled the kilns that were once brightly burning beacons. Patterns on the ground were all that was left of the cart tracks, and the dusty spoil heaps grew to resemble grassy hillocks.

All that remain today to bear witness to human ingenuity and endeavour are the fragmented scars of a defunct industry. Now the silence of the unsullied, peaceful moorland is broken only by the haunting call of the curlew.

A collier and his donkey cart, photographed near Ingleton

# WALK 12

## WEASDALE, RANDYGILL TOP AND GREEN BELL

**DIFFICULTY** 👢 👢 👢   **DISTANCE** 7½ miles (12 km)

| WATH | LEATHGILL BRIDGE | RANDYGILL TOP | GREEN BELL | RAVENSTONE-DALE COMMON | WEASDALE | WATH |

**MAPS** OS Explorer OL19, Howgill Fells and Upper Eden Valley, or Harveys Howgill Fells Superwalker

**STARTING POINT** The Bowderdale/Wath exit off the A685 (GR 684050)

**PUBLIC TRANSPORT** Stagecoach bus service 564 runs from Penrith and Kendal to Newbiggin on Lune, approximately 1 mile (1.6 km) east of the start point (Monday–Saturday; telephone 0870 6082608 for times).

**PARKING** Along the verges of the access lanes either side of the A685

A route offering a variety of scenery and terrain, from the steep ascent up Randygill Top to the gentle woods and pastures around Weasdale. For the most part elevated, with great views.

■ Although now just a small farming community, at one time Wath (meaning ford) was a sizeable hamlet which grew in importance as it stood where an old cattle drovers' road forded the River Lune. The road came from the north over Crosby Garrett

Fell and Ravenstonedale Moor, past Rigg End and across the Lune at Wath, before proceeding south along Bowderdale to eventually reach the Rawthey valley. A low bridge under the A685 still allows for the movement of cattle.

From 1861 until its closure in the 1960s, the Kirkby Stephen–Tebay line also came this way, running down Smardale a little to the east of here. The name of the station at Newbiggin on Lune was changed to Ravenstonedale to avoid confusion with the station at Newbiggin near Stainton in the Lune valley on the Settle–Carlisle line. Parish records recall that you could sometimes get a haircut at Ravenstonedale station.

A more modern route near here is the Pennine Cycleway, which covers the 350 miles (560 km) from Derby up to Berwick-upon-Tweed. As Route 68, the cycleway forms part of the National Cycle Network of safe and attractive routes co-ordinated by the charity Sustrans. Route 68 links the two main areas covered by this book as it passes between the Three Peaks and up the western edge of the Howgill Fells.

▶ Head west along the southern access road, to quickly join a lane heading south, signposted Scar Sikes. At GR 678035 **1**, take the left track swinging away from the wall. Climb straight up Hooksey and carry on in the same direction along a tractor track (a little indistinct in places), to drop down to Leathgill Bridge.

■ Leathgill Bridge isn't what's normally thought of as a bridge; it's a totally natural phenomenon and a splendid example of a narrow saddle rising to span a deep valley. It allows passage between the valleys of Weasdale and Bowderdale, saving the walker from a much deeper descent and ascent. It's a windy spot, but cross with gratitude.

▶ Follow the faint trod going straight up to the cairn on the summit of Randygill Top **2**.

■ Away to the north the fells near Crosby Garrett can be seen. They are crossed by Wainwright's Coast to Coast Walk, the celebrated traverse of Britain from St Bees (near Whitehaven) on the Irish Sea to Robin Hood's Bay by the North Sea.

▶ Swing left over Stockless, another saddle, to reach the trig point on Green Bell ❸.

■ The elevated walk between the grassy summits of Randygill Top and Green Bell offers superb views, the stunning panorama extending for miles in all directions. Near by are the valleys of Ravenstonedale and Wandale. On a good day, you can see the Eden valley, the outline of the Pennines, Wild Boar Fell, Baugh Fell with the hills above Wensleydale and Wharefedale beyond, Ingleborough, Whernside and the Lakeland fells.

Dale Gill, the headwater of the River Lune, rises from a spring on the eastern flank of Green Bell. The watershed between the Lune and the River Eden is just a little further east, between Newbiggin and Ravenstonedale.

▶ Keep on the obvious path over Ravenstonedale Common to GR 696028 ❹, just before Pinskey Head. Work left to pick up a track running around the outside of the intake wall and follow it until it meets a lane. Turn left and walk to the T-junction at Weasdale Farm.

■ The family at Weasdale Farm is the longest continuing line living in the same house in Ravenstonedale parish. In 1774, the family was granted permission from the manor of Ravenstonedale to 'one cattle-gate in a common field, for a rent of eightpence per annum'.

The Lane, a house just to the north of Weasdale, was built by Thomas Hewetson who, according to local folklore, went to London with £100 in his pocket in 1839 to make his fortune. He started a furniture business on Tottenham Court Road and was bought out twenty years later by the firm that was to become Maples. This made him a wealthy man and he built The Lane in 1860, adorning the interior walls with fashionable stencil work and London's most exotic wallpapers.

▶ Turn right by the farm to walk through the land of Weasdale Nurseries **5**.

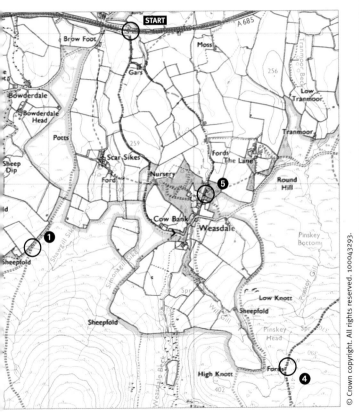

▶ Map continues southwards on page 153

■ Weasdale Nurseries started business in 1952 and, at an altitude of 850 ft (260 m), is one of the highest nurseries in Britain. Its mail order service offers a diverse range of extremely hardy trees and shrubs, sending them all over the country and occasionally to Europe. Stock is grown in the open ground, not in containers, which means plants are sold bare-rooted in the dormant season between November and early spring.

The established woodland here contrasts sharply with the surrounding open fell and meadowlands. The diversity of the nursery's stock, coupled with the variety of woodland that shelters it, has encouraged a range of wildlife to take advantage of the habitat. Although threatened from all sides by the invasive grey squirrels, there's a steady population of red squirrels living around the nursery (see page 134), and roe deer also seek safety among the trees. Some of the less-common birds seen at Weasdale are merlin, woodcock, shrike, meadow pipit, redstart and firecrest. The owners of the nursery welcome walkers to look around as they pass through.

▶ Keep the beck to your left, then cross it at a footbridge and continue north across the meadows past Gars. Exit on to the A685 by crossing another footbridge, then turn left and walk the short distance along the grass verge back to the start point.

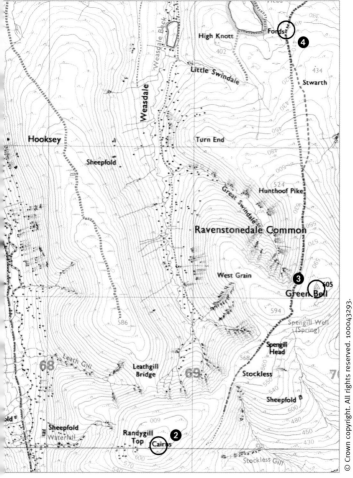

# Some further reading

Here is a small selection of books which will tell you more about the area. Please note that not all are still in print.

Bruce Bedford, *Underground Britain*, Collins, 1985

Barry Cockcroft, *The Dale that Died*, Dent, 1975

Dr John Hamilton, *Mallerstang Dale*, Broadcast Books, 1993

Marie Hartley and Joan Ingilby, *The Old Hand-Knitters of the Dales*, Dalesman, 1951

Marie Hartley and Joan Ingilby, *The Yorkshire Dales*, new edition Smith Settle, 1991

Phil Hudson, *Coal Mining in Lunesdale*, Hudson History, 1998

W.R. Mitchell, *Garsdale*, Castleberg, 1999

W.R. Mitchell, *High Dale Country*, Souvenir Press, 1991

Frederick Riley, *Gleanings from an Old-world Hamlet*, The Book Stores, Settle, n.d.

Tom Stephenson, *Forbidden Land*, Ramblers' Association, 1989

Tom Stephenson, *The Pennine Way*, HMSO, 1969

A. Wainwright, *On the Pennine Way*, Michael Joseph, 1985

A. Wainwright, *Walks in Limestone Country*, new edition Frances Lincoln, 2003

Dr A.A. Wilson, *Geology of the Yorkshire Dales National Park*, The Yorkshire Dales National Park Committee, 1975

Geoffrey Wright, *Roads and Trackways of the Yorkshire Dales*, Moorland Publishing, 1985

# The Countryside Code

An abbreviated version of the Countryside Code, launched in 2004 and supported by a wide range of countryside organizations including the Ramblers' Association, is given below.

### Be safe – plan ahead and follow signs

Even when going out locally, it's best to get the latest information about where and when you can go; for example, your rights to enter some areas of open land may be restricted while work is being carried out, for safety reasons or during breeding seasons. Follow advice and local signs, and be prepared for the unexpected.

### Leave gates and property as you find them

Please respect the working life of the countryside, as our actions can affect rural livelihoods, the safety and welfare of animals and people, and the heritage that belongs to all of us.

### Protect plants and animals, and take your litter home

We have a responsibility to protect the countryside now and for future generations, so make sure you don't harm animals, birds, plants or trees.

### Keep dogs under control

The countryside is a great place to exercise dogs, but it's every owner's duty to make sure their dog is not a danger or nuisance to farm animals, wildlife or other people.

### Consider other people

Showing consideration and respect for other people makes the countryside a pleasant environment for everyone, whether they are at home, at work or at leisure.

# Index

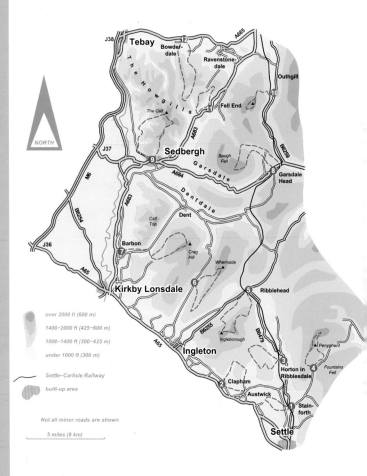

NORTH

over 2000 ft (600 m)

1400–2000 ft (425–600 m)

1000–1400 ft (300–425 m)

under 1000 ft (300 m)

Settle–Carlisle Railway

built-up area

Not all minor roads are shown

5 miles (8 km)